"*Turning the Tables* is pure crack for foodies looking for more 'inside' information on the restaurant world. Knowledgeable, helpful (particularly in the section on how to order sushi), and always opinionated, Shaw knows what the hell he's talking about. I enjoyed every page—even when I disagreed with him."　　—Anthony Bourdain, author of *Kitchen Confidential*

"In his penetrating first book, restaurant critic and food columnist Shaw decodes the secrets of the food world. Driven by his passion for food, he goes behind the scenes—often undercover—to do prep work in restaurant kitchens, tour farms and markets with food buyers and produce managers, and even make an early-morning stop at the Fulton Fish Market in New York City to trace the ingredients of a meal to a diner's plate. . . . After this vicarious romp, readers will gain new confidence in their abilities to choose restaurants, make—and get—coveted reservations, decipher menus, and order great meals. . . . A delicious read for restaurant goers."
　　　　　　　　　　　　　　　　　　　　　　—*Library Journal*

"Sound, neighborly advice on getting reservations . . . briskly tough . . . and quite courageous in his assaults on the *Times*' reviewing."
　　　　　　　　　　　　　　　　　　　　　　—*The New Yorker*

"Shaw can be counted on for the funny, blunt, and sometimes controversial opinions that have helped make him a heavyweight in the culinary world."　　　　　　　　　　　　　　　　　　—*Chicago Sun-Times*

"'The Fat Guy' makes his case. . . . *Turning the Tables* is a well-rounded work by a well-rounded guy."　　　　　　　　　　　　—*Boston Globe*

"Shaw knows a lot about restaurants and how they work, so he provides a lot of interesting and useful information. Moreover, he's not a food snob; a hot-dog stand in Connecticut gets as much applause from him as an expensive, trendy vendor of haute cuisine in Manhattan."
　　　　　　　　　　—Jonathan Yardley, *Washington Post Book World*

"Shaw dissects everything from reservation systems—scarily specific these days, some track favorite tables, no-shows, even how strong to brew your tea—to restaurant reviews and the intricate path your food takes to the table."　　　　　　　　　　　　　　　　　　　—*Fortune*

"Steven Shaw tells you how to get exceptional service every time."
　　　　　　　　　　　　　　　　　　　　　　—*Newsweek*

"Steven Shaw's *Turning the Tables* takes the reader behind the scenes and shows how restaurants run and how one's dining experience can be maximized. . . . A mixture of avuncular advice ('If you don't like a table, say so before you sit down') and sociological observations."   —*New York Sun*

"Anyone thinking of going to culinary school needs to read *Turning the Tables* before writing the first tuition check."   —*Florida Times-Union*

"A mixed bag of advice, insider information, and soapboxing (on everything from organic food and 'authentic cuisine' to restaurant critics), this opinionated diner's tour is sure to appeal to chowhounds in general and New Yorkers in particular."   —*Publishers Weekly*

"Hanging out with the reservationist (yes, he assures the reader, it is a word), assisting in the kitchen of Manhattan's renowned Gramercy Tavern, and counting the number of eggs used on a Sunday at the Tavern on the Green, Shaw darts into those exalted places that most foodies only conjecture about, and he soaks up the atmosphere for hours and days at a time. . . . Solid work."   —*Kirkus Reviews*

"*Turning the Tables* is packed with useful information. An enjoyable guide through the restaurant world, it can make an amateur eater into an expert who knows how to snag a table at a top restaurant and what to do when he gets there."   —*Daily News*

"Shaw, who has earned the respect of both restaurant staffs and other critics, is an accomplished advocate for restaurant patrons and a firm believer in the democratic nature of even the greatest dining establishments."
—*Albany Times Union*

"Shaw writes with humor, passion, and an abiding love for eating well. His curiosity fuels his arguments and he wants others to share in his joy of the meal."
—*Nashville Tennessean*

"In *Turning the Tables*, Steven Shaw proves to be (1) a genial blunderbuss, (2) a shoe fetishist, (3) a keen-eyed writer, (4) a contrary critic, and (5) a restaurant-goer's ideal advocate and ombudsman."
—John T. Edge, author of *Hamburgers & Fries: An American Story*

"Chefs and restaurateurs should be warned that the jig is up. eGullet's prolific and savvy, irreverent Fat Guy has told all their secrets, with enough tips on inner workings to enable even the least celebrated restaurant buffs to get their money's worth at the hottest, snootiest joints. Not only that, he has done it with great style and humor, making this a delicious read."
—Mimi Sheraton, author of *Eating My Words*

Ellen R. Shapiro

About the Author

STEVEN A. SHAW, a.k.a. "The Fat Guy," is the founder of the phenomenally successful eGullet Web site, a James Beard Award–winning food critic, and a contributor to *Elle, Saveur,* and many other magazines and journals. He is the perfect guide for novices and pros alike when it comes to getting the best a restaurant has to offer, starting with those all-important, impossible-to-get reservations. Named by *Food & Wine* as one of the thirty-five most fearsome young talents in food, he is incorruptible, irreverent, and often controversial.

Turning

the

Tables

*The Insider's Guide
to Eating Out*

Steven A. Shaw

HARPER

NEW YORK · LONDON · TORONTO · SYDNEY

For Ellen, who drives me

HARPER

A hardcover edition of this book was published in 2005 by HarperCollins Publishers.

TURNING THE TABLES. Copyright © 2005 by Steven A. Shaw. All rights reserved. Printed in the United States of America. No part of this book may be used or reproduced in any manner whatsoever without written permission except in the case of brief quotations embodied in critical articles and reviews. For information address HarperCollins Publishers, 10 East 53rd Street, New York, NY 10022.

HarperCollins books may be purchased for educational, business, or sales promotional use. For information please write: Special Markets Department, HarperCollins Publishers, 10 East 53rd Street, New York, NY 10022.

First Harper paperback published 2006.

Designed by Joseph Rutt

The Library of Congress has catalogued the hardcover edition as follows:
Shaw, Steven (Steven A.).
    Turning the tables : restaurants from the inside out / Steven A. Shaw
      p. cm.
    Includes bibliographical references and index.
   ISBN 0-06-073780-8
   1. Restaurants. I. Title.
TX911.S43 2005
647.95—dc22   2004061575

ISBN-10: 0-06-089140-8
ISBN-13: 978-0-06-089140-4

06 07 08 09 10 ❖/RRD 10 9 8 7 6 5 4 3 2 1

ACKNOWLEDGMENTS

To the people in the restaurant business and related industries who gave of their time and knowledge; to my editor, Susan Friedland, and her assistants, Califia Suntree and Rupa Bhattacharya, who turned a manuscript into a book; to my agent Michael Psaltis, who believed in me; to the magazine and newspaper editors, especially Neal Kozodoy at *Commentary* and Dorothy Hughes at the *New York Law Journal*, who helped me develop several of the ideas and arguments that have come together in this book; to Wayne and Julie Shovelin, who gave their lake house as a safe haven for writing; to my technology guru Jason Perlow, the Linux community, and the OpenOffice organization, who gave me a year of writing without a single crash; to the members and staff of the eGullet Society, especially Dave Scantland for suggesting the title; to my trio of life advisors, Prof. Richard Sugarman (philosophical), Dr. Neil Altman (psychological), and the Ven. Jinmyo Renge (spiritual); to Ken Matthews, who always pays for dinner; to my mother, Penny Shaw, who took it well when I said I was becoming a writer; to Nick Jordan, who always has a kind word; to my sister, Jennifer Shaw, who helped me rewrite, and rewrite again; to my bulldog, Momo, who kept vigil at my side during all those long nights of writing; to my wife, Ellen Shapiro, who is my support network, my best reader, my uncredited collaborator, the only friend I need, and after all this time I've spent working on the book perhaps the only friend I have left; and to my late father, Peter Shaw, who taught me how to dine:
Thank you.

Contents

Why I Love Restaurants

Some would say I became a food critic to subsidize a restaurant addiction. They would be right. But my condition is probably genetic.

Three decades before the current restaurant-architecture trend of "open kitchen" design (which typically allows customers to see a restaurant's cooks at work behind glass), before *Kitchen Confidential* and *The Restaurant* reality show, and before Food TV was a gleam in its creators' eyes, my father used to take me every weekend to the original open kitchen: the breakfast griddle at the local diner.

We spent countless hours over a period of years watching the griddle man, and all the while my father delivered a ceaseless stream of commentary: "You see, son," he would say, "he does the home fries the right way—with baked potatoes. Now, pay attention while he does that big table's order. He's got to have all six dishes ready at the same time. Only the best cooks can do that every time. This man was a plasma physicist back in Russia, you know."

My memories of dining with my father have set the tone for my whole attitude toward and passion for restaurants.

Dining with him wasn't only about the food—it was about people, about ideas, and especially about building an inventory of inside jokes. Once, a little old lady came into the diner and asked for liver and onions.

"Cut it up in little pieces," she demanded.

"Cut it up in little pieces," the Russian physicist/griddle man replied, with a bow.

"Cut it up in little pieces," added my father, gratuitously, from the other end of the counter.

It became an inside joke for us that lasted twenty years. Even as my father lay exhausted on his deathbed, in the final round of his decade-long fight against heart disease, I was able to elicit a smile from him by whispering, "Cut it up in little pieces."

As he did with respect to all areas of human endeavor, my father had more than his fair share of theories about restaurants. "You can't get good service in an empty restaurant," he used to say, since vitality is crucial to a restaurant's performance. A literature professor, he analyzed menus with the same intellectual rigor he applied to the great books and, through such analysis, was unfailing in his ability to select the best dishes. He was fond of saying, "I'd rather have the Stage Deli name a sandwich after me than win the Nobel Prize."

Even when eating a hamburger at midnight, an indulgence he permitted himself once a month, my father could be overheard quoting Shakespeare and Melville in his conversation with the fry cook. Waiters at the neighborhood restaurants called him "The Professor." They would seek his advice on marital problems and ask him questions about the nature of being. My father treated the lowliest bathroom-mopper as an intellectual equal. I used to stare at him incredulously when he would try to explain Dostoyevsky to the Greek ex-con dishwasher at a restaurant on the corner of 69th and Broadway in Manhattan. "This man," my father would patiently explain to me, "may very well be a descendant of Aristotle (or Confucius, or Leonardo da Vinci). Can you and I claim such honorable ancestry?" My father often spoke like he was reading from a book.

At holiday time, he and I would walk around the neighborhood and, with great ceremony, he would present a crisp twenty-dollar bill to his favorite waiters at each of his regular haunts. The waiters would grasp the bills as though they were the crown jewels. It wasn't the money they were reacting to—it was the thought, the fanfare, the connection to a different era and attitude. He always called waiters by name and he always asked a million questions about their homes, their families, and their heritage. And he remembered every answer, because every answer was important to him.

My father never managed to get a sandwich named after him at the Stage Deli, and he never won the Nobel Prize. Years after his death, however, a Greek diner on Columbus Avenue still offers "The Professor Salad," and you can still order "Professor's Special Lobster Cantonese" at a local Chinese restaurant. And I like to think that, somewhere out there, the Russian grill man is teaching physics at a prestigious university but still remembers how to make "Eggs Professor."

We were a family with a middle-class income—both of my parents were teachers. As a teen, my idea of a fancy meal was the monthly visit to Gallagher's steakhouse in the Broadway theater district with my father and my uncle

Paul. By the time I was a teenager, I was cooking dinner for my friends on the Stuyvesant High School debating team—sometimes ten or more of them at a time. In college I was considered something of an oddball because I cooked so much of my own food and would walk an hour or more in the Vermont winter to visit the only good Chinese restaurant near Burlington, housed in what I think used to be a Kentucky Fried Chicken in an office-building parking lot on a lonely stretch of Shelburne Road. I married the girl who always walked with me.

It was in my second year of law school at Fordham University in New York that I discovered fine dining, courtesy of the many law firms that came to my school to recruit young lawyers-to-be for their summer associate programs. A half-day interview with several partners would be capped off by lunch at a fine restaurant with a group of the firm's younger associates. The legal hiring process, overseen by an organization called NALP, allowed me to schedule fifty job interviews. Even though I planned to accept an offer from the first firm that had interviewed me, which had been my top choice, I kept the other forty-nine appointments so I could get the free lunches. Whichever fool said there's no such thing as a free lunch never interviewed for a law firm job.

My first assignment as a commercial litigator at a large midtown Manhattan law firm began the day after my wife and I returned from our honeymoon. My boss, Rory Millson, called the night before: "Shaw, it's Millson. Come early tomorrow. Bring clothes."

The trial had me living in a hotel and working out of temporary offices in Wilmington, Delaware, toiling 24/7 for almost nine weeks. True to my nature, though, over the course of my incarceration in Wilmington, I sussed out all the best places to eat and, in what turned out to be the beginning of my next career, I wrote a short Wilmington restaurant survival guide, which became a bit of a cult classic around the New York law firm scene. To this day someone will occasionally e-mail me a copy and ask, "Hey, did you really write this? Your writing used to suck!"

As an attorney I was well paid, but if you divided the number of hours I worked each year into my salary I was probably paid less than my secretary. My wife, Ellen, and I, who as students had become accustomed to 24/7 access to one another, now had to schedule "date nights," and we had a standing Saturday lunch date at a favorite restaurant, the now-defunct Lespinasse.

Lespinasse was one of my formative fine-dining experiences. Most of my fine dining at that time had occurred as a result of my getting involved in big law firm culture, so I was fairly new to restaurants like Lespinasse. Still, I had been to most of the big-name places by then and I thought I understood good food. That was until eight of us, including the head of the firm, went for dinner at Lespinasse, and my eyes were opened. It was an awakening. I was so astounded by the food, the surroundings (Lespinasse looked like a palace ballroom), and the service (I learned years later that our waiter's name was Karl) that I barely participated in the dinner conversation and, instead, held a hushed dialogue with Karl about each dish, each glass of wine, and each utensil. I knew I would be back.

Over time, and with my meals at Lespinasse and many other restaurants in mind, I realized I was more interested in my business lunches than in my business as a lawyer. I started to write short restaurant reviews and food essays, and I sent them around to magazines and newspapers, hoping to get them published. After about a year of that, during which time I didn't get a single thing published, I turned to the Internet. It was just around the time when, with a bit of effort and study, any crackpot with delusions of grandeur could create and maintain a basic Web site. This crackpot put fifty restaurant reviews online and waited.

At first, only my friends in the law business, a few hard-core Internet junkies, and my mother read the site. Then one day the *New York Times* discovered my reviews and discussed the site in a food section article. Overnight, my site went from getting about twenty visitors per day to getting more than twenty thousand. I remember my Internet service provider e-mailing me that day: "We suspect your Web site may be under attack."

New Media outlets such as Salon.com and the now-defunct Sidewalk.com picked up on my work and, later, so did newspapers and magazines. But working full time as an attorney, I didn't have the time to hone my craft. So I made a choice: I gave up my career as a lawyer in order to devote my life to writing about food.

Over a five-year period, I wrote more than five hundred restaurant reviews. They mostly followed the standard format: a discussion of the various dishes on the menu, plus commentary on the decor, service, ambience, and wine list. Ultimately, though, I found that restaurant reviews were a limited form of expression, because they answer only the most basic *Consumer Reports* level of inquiry: "Where should I eat?" And they answer it in the most generic way, from a reductionistic dish-by-dish perspective. I felt there were plenty of restaurant reviews out there, but that there was something missing. I began to focus my writing on larger issues, not so much where to eat, but how to dine.

On my thirtieth birthday, Ellen took me to dinner at Gramercy Tavern in New York City, then and now one of my favorite restaurants. Our waiter, Christopher Russell, who went on to become the beverage and service director at the legendary Union Square Cafe, overheard bits and pieces of our conversation and finally asked, "Are you Steven Shaw, the Internet food guy?" It was the first time anybody had ever recognized me as a writer. The chef, Tom Colicchio—who apparently had also been reading my work—came to the table and introduced himself.

My moment of glory was cut short, however, by a pronouncement from Colicchio. "You know what's wrong with your writing?" he asked. "It's that you have absolutely no idea what happens on the other side of the kitchen doors."

I blanched. I sputtered. I recovered. I challenged: "So what are you going to do about it?"

"Come in Monday at 9 A.M. Ask for my sous-chef, Matt Seeber. I'll order a cook's jacket in your size."

That week in the Gramercy Tavern kitchen, in addition to being murder on my feet, raised my addiction to a new level. I dedicated myself to learning as much as I could about every aspect of the business, from the inside out: all the things one doesn't see as a consumer. I hit up two other chefs—Christian Delouvrier and Alain Ducasse—for kitchen time. I shopped with chefs. I visited farmers and fishermen. I spent time with waitstaff. A lot of time. And not just in fancy restaurants. I'm equally fascinated by temples of haute cuisine and roadside barbecue joints, by the most exclusive Japanese restaurants and the local pizzerias with their "stick men" who manipulate the pizzas with long wooden peels. I've spent the past several years investigating every level of restaurant, from New York to Vancouver and from Chicago to the Southeast, from the special-occasion place to the business-lunch spot to the local frankfurter stand. Though restaurants are infinitely diverse, when viewed in an operational sense restaurants at every level appear quite similar. Like any two species of the same genus, the genetic codes of the highest and lowest restaurants in America have far more in common than not.

My goal in writing this book is to take you on an insider's guided tour of the world of restaurant dining, from farm to table and from the birth of a restaurant concept through opening day and beyond. This book is the result of quite a lot of investigation, but it is emphatically not an exposé. It is, rather, a celebration of everything there is to love about restaurants. I know that people have many fears about restaurants—sanitation code violations, shady business practices, exploitation of ignorance—and too many journalists take the easy route by playing into those fears. Certainly, as in any business, there are some unsavory characters in the restaurant industry. And there are plenty of bad restaurants. But they are not my focus.

There is much to be celebrated: the meal you eat in a restaurant is the end result of a process that begins on the farm, on the balance sheet, and in the minds of the chef and restaurateur. The twelve million employees in the $440 billion U.S. restaurant industry—it is the second largest employer in the nation, after the government—toil day and night in 878,000 restaurants to make your 70 billion annual restaurant meals seem effortless. But they're not: even the most modest restaurant meal is the conclusion of a lengthy chain of events. To me, it's more remarkable than sending a man to the moon.

The sequence of bringing food from its source to your plate can be as simple as a local farmer dropping off a box of tomatoes at the restaurant's back door, but it usually involves an international network: a calf destined for the table at a restaurant in Philadelphia may have been raised in Canada. At the slaughterhouse, even outside the United States, inspectors from the U.S. Department of Agriculture are on hand to certify the wholesomeness of any carcasses destined for these shores. Shipping by refrigerated rail, truck, or ship must be coordinated by the logistics industry, itself a worthy subject for a book. The carcasses may then arrive at a distribution center, where they are butchered into different cuts and shipped off to wholesalers, who then move the product to restaurants, hotels, cafeterias, supermarkets, and any other end-user who wants a large piece of meat. Most larger restaurants have their own butchers on staff to cut and trim the meat into individual portions. Between the butcher, the cooks, and the food runner who brings you your plate of food, it's not unusual for a piece of meat to pass through six or seven different people's custody before it is served.

The farm-to-table sequence of events is, however, only one of many strands of activity that lead up to your dining experience. Someone also has to create the restaurant: an idea is born, financing is arranged, an architect and a designer create the physical concept, construction begins, publicists and consultants work to generate pre-opening buzz, cooks, waitstaff, and managers are hired, flatware, crystal, china, linens, chairs, tables, artwork, vases, and all manner of accessory are purchased, the wine cellar and bar are stocked, reservations are taken, the restaurant opens, the newspaper and magazine critics arrive and review it, Internet foodies share their early meal reports, and eventually the restaurant establishes its clientele, or it doesn't.

Virtually every aspect of contemporary society is somehow touched by the restaurant industry, and many of the burning issues of the day have an impact on or are affected by our dining choices. The agricultural practices of ingredients suppliers reflect decisions about the genetic modification of foodstuffs and critical issues of public health law ranging from pasteurization of milk to mad-cow disease. Tipping, which is the primary system of compensation for waitstaff, touches on fundamental labor concerns. In the media, restaurant reviews illustrate the relationship between critics, consumers, and businesses. Modern restaurant culture is a point on a continuum with a past, present, and future, and the history of cuisine reflects the history of our culture.

Although the restaurant business is connected to all aspects of American life, the world of restaurants is also a world unto itself—larger than the entire nation of Belgium, Greece, Hungary, or Portugal—with its own language and laws, some written and some unwritten. Those in the business refer to the rest of us as "civilians." Restaurant work is "The Life."

Twenty years ago, people didn't know or care who was cooking and serving their food; the attitude was "just bring me my food and shut up." Times have changed.

Restaurants and chefs are fast becoming more central to American culture: witness the success of the Zagat guides and the continued rise of Food TV. Culinary school is the new law school; with enrollment on the rise, there are more chefs, more restaurants, and more opportunities to eat better in every city.

Though understanding how restaurants work is fascinating in and of itself, and though informed food choices can greatly enrich one's life, there's another benefit to acquiring this knowledge of the inner workings of the business: by better understanding how restaurants work, we can also learn how better to enjoy dining in them. If you speak the language of restaurants, you can get what you want: better service, food, reservations, and overall experience. With restaurants demystified, you will read a menu, a restaurant review, or any kind of restaurant guide in a new light, separating the wheat from the chaff, seeing past the agendas, and zeroing in on the good information buried within. Understanding the inner workings of the restaurant business can help you pick the right restaurants for every occasion, know the limits of your reasonable expectations at different types of restaurants, and protect your wallet from needless expenditures.

I see this book as following the evolution of a love for and command of restaurant dining, from the inside out and the outside in. It begins with a dawn 'til dusk chronicle of what a restaurant's service staff does, along with brass-tacks advice on getting what you want in restaurants. Then it takes you behind the kitchen doors and into the world of food sources and controversies. It critiques the critics and the guidebooks, encouraging you to form your own opinions based on your needs and preferences. It reveals the business side of restaurants, from the birth of a new restaurant to the ways successful operators manage restaurant empires. In the end, it looks back at how restaurant culture developed and looks forward to what I hope will be a bright restaurant future.

If you're new to restaurant dining, I hope this book serves as your introduction. If you already love to dine, I hope this book helps you love it more. Because I firmly believe that if you love restaurants for the right reasons, they will love you back.

Turning
the
Tables

CHAPTER ONE

Getting What You Want

As you walk down the corridor toward a restaurant's exit, restroom, or patio, they're always there in your peripheral vision: the doors. Most every restaurant has a few blank doors; you're not really supposed to notice them. What's going on behind those doors?

At New York's Eleven Madison Park, Isabel Rodriguez is behind one of those doors, taking reservations. When it comes to getting reservations, Isabel can be your best friend. Or not.

When you call for a reservation at most fine-dining restaurants today, the phone isn't answered by a tuxedoed maitre d' standing at a podium. He doesn't inscribe your reservation in the pages of a substantial leather tome. Rather, your call is likely to be answered by a reservation-ist—it's not in your dictionary, but it's a word—sitting in an office, and her tools will be a headset, a multiline telephone, and a computer.

At exactly 9 A.M., Isabel activates the phones (if you call earlier, you'll just get a recorded message) and within a few seconds four lines are ringing. "Eleven Madison Park, would you please hold? Thank you!" she says four times in succession, in a faintly accented English reminiscent of a James Bond seductress. As she gets back to the first caller, her hands are a blur of mouseclicks and keystrokes as she decisively navigates the electronic reservation system to a date, time, and table size, all the while acting as though there's no pressure from the other three (and soon four) callers standing by.

As soon as Isabel keys in the first few letters of the caller's last name, if he has reserved before, the OpenTable software starts narrowing the choices from its database. After four letters it's down to one choice, and Isabel knows the caller's first name before he even gives it. And she knows more: not only his phone number, but also a dossier of information that would make the Central Intelligence Agency drool. At more and more restaurants, "guest management" software like OpenTable is used to keep records of everything from allergies to birthdays.

This particular customer has been to the restaurant seventeen times before, and there is a record of all those dates. He has also made two reservations that he subsequently canceled. He has zero no-shows. The servers and managers have picked up various information and entered it into the computer over time: He works in the office building adjacent to the restaurant. He prefers to sit in section 3 of the dining room, preferably in a corner. One time he sent back his tea because it wasn't strong enough, so there's a notation "brew tea very strong."

Not every call is for a reservation. Someone wants to purchase a gift certificate; Isabel faxes her a request form. Other callers want to arrange private parties, speak to restaurant employees, apply for jobs—Isabel's hands dance across the phone's controls as she transfers each call to the right place. In her moments of downtime, Isabel wraps chocolate maple leaf candies for a charity event in which the restaurant is participating, types up special event menus, and answers my questions. During the three days I observe Isabel in action, I never see her performing fewer than two tasks at once.

Eleven Madison Park is a busy restaurant, and getting a prime-time reservation on a weekend night can be a challenge. Some people get those reservations, and others don't. As this chapter demonstrates, as we watch The Life unfold from morning until the wee hours, the flip side of knowing what Isabel's job entails is knowing how to work with her to get the reservations you want. Watching Isabel at work and listening to dozens of her phone calls confirms that whether or not you get that empty table is very much up to you.

Every night at a popular restaurant is like an overbooked airline flight. And restaurants, like airlines, operate on razor-thin profit margins; a couple of empty seats can mean the difference between profit and loss for the evening. Most restaurants that accept reservations therefore overbook their dining rooms, because they know that a certain percentage of the reservations will either cancel late in the game or be no-shows at the moment of truth. And in the end, after all the cancellations and no-shows have been tallied, there is almost always an empty table. Your mission, should you choose to accept it? Get that empty table.

Whether you really want or need that table is, however, an open question. Too many people, I think, place too much emphasis on visiting restaurants that are new, hot, staffed by a celebrity chef, featured on Food TV, or otherwise in demand, rather than restaurants that are simply good. Although my work as a food journalist often requires that I visit hard-to-book restaurants—and thus I've become extremely facile when it comes to getting in—when spending my own money I prefer to go to restaurants that are tried and true.

Should you wish to get into an in-demand restaurant, however, the first step is to acquire a basic understanding of restaurant demographics, which includes a good working knowledge of local news, weather, and even sports. The most painless way to get a reservation is to take a cue from the judo masters: never fight strength with strength. Instead, be a contrarian. If the restaurant does mostly dinner business, go for lunch (the food will be the same, and often cheaper). If it serves a mostly pretheater crowd, go at 8 P.M. If it's a business-oriented place, go on the weekend. Even the most popular restaurants tend to be empty during blizzards, the Superbowl, and Monica Lewinsky's Barbara Walters interview.

But sometimes you don't want to eat at 5:30 P.M. on a Tuesday, or in a snowstorm. What then? The lesson I've learned from observing Isabel and interacting with scores of other reservationists over the years is that, when attempting to secure a reservation for the busiest times, the key is polite but confident persistence. Remember the pathetic guy in high school who asked every girl out on a date and never gave up in the face of repeated rejection? Remember your astonishment at his lack of self-respect? Remember how, one day, he scored? When it comes to reservations, you want to be like that guy. It's that careful balance between genuine enthusiasm, flattery, and exhaustion that makes extra seats magically open up. In the world of Eleven Madison Park, you want to be the person who gets Isabel to like you enough to make the reservations computer work hard on your behalf.

Most people, when told a restaurant is "fully committed," will give up. But if you're fully committed to getting a reservation, the first phone call is only the beginning. Everybody wants to be wanted, so you need to communicate your desire to the reservationist, sometimes repeatedly. Let that person know you care enough about dining at the restaurant that you're not going to give up until you get a table—maybe not at that time or even on that day, but you're going to get one. If your first attempt is rejected, start asking questions. Is there a waiting list? When does the restaurant require confirmations? When does the restaurant get most of its cancellations? (Usually right around the time confirmations are required, and also during the afternoon the day of.) What are the reservationist's hopes, dreams, and favorite kind of dog?

If you must, call every day and become the reservationist's best friend. As my friend Kelly Alexander, an editor at *Saveur* magazine, puts it, "Talk to the reservationist as if he or she was God. Get the person on your side by being absolutely amenable."

There are few restaurants in the world where you won't be able to get in by using the aforementioned techniques. Still, every good strategy must have several contingency plans, and in some extreme cases—such as at the most popular places in large cities on weekend nights—you may very well fail at getting an advance reservation. But hope is not lost.

Given how many people cancel their reservations at the

last minute or fail to confirm them, an ironic situation arises: it's often easier to get a reservation the day of than it is to get one a month in advance. So find out from the reservationist when the restaurant requires confirmations, and call one minute after the deadline. Ask when the bulk of day-of cancellations typically come in—depending on the restaurant this could be anywhere from noon to right before the dinner service—and call around that time. And make sure the reservationst remembers that you're the nice couple from Arizona, or the woman who just loves the chef's sweetbreads, or in my case the guy with the English bulldog named Momo.

Even if you can't get a last-minute reservation, if you simply must dine at a particular restaurant I recommend you just show up. Once you're on the inside, don't give up until the last cook goes home for the night. It is almost inconceivable that a neatly dressed, polite potential customer, sitting at a restaurant's bar and exhibiting a willingness to wait and a desire to experience and pay for a restaurant's cuisine, will not eventually be given a table. So far I have never failed with this strategy, though I've endured some long evenings. (Those long evenings are great times to collect gossip from bartenders, though.)

There are a few folks out there who will say they have reservations when they don't. I see it from time to time in restaurants, and it creates a terribly awkward situation for the restaurant's staff. Worse, it casts a shadow over those who truly find themselves in the position of having a reservation misplaced by a restaurant, something that should never happen in the age of computers and confirmations, but that occasionally does.

By noon, Isabel is making some phone calls of her own.

Eleven Madison Park informs customers making reservations that, the day before a reservation, they should call the restaurant to confirm. Some customers don't follow through on this commitment, so Isabel calls them. After three calls in a row during which the customer gives a response along the lines of, "Oh, I won't be coming, thanks," Isabel, who has been exceedingly polite on the phone, says to me, "What do these people think they're doing? I have a waiting list of people who really want to eat here, and I have people holding reservations that they're not going to use." Some of those people, moreover, may be holding reservations at multiple restaurants for the same evening and are planning to make a last-minute decision about which reservation to honor. Isabel recovers quickly and is back to her cheerful self, making another round of calls. Reservationists tend to be resilient.

Failing to confirm or honor a reservation is not only inconsiderate, but also puts a strain on the system that results in delay, disappointment, and confusion for other customers. Now that you are a whiz at getting reservations, there is a corresponding responsibility that comes with that power: you need to play by the rules and confirm and keep your reservations. Moreover, you need to be respectful of the process: don't hold multiple reservations until the last minute. Here, as in much of life, let the golden rule be your guide.

Several years ago, I ate dinner at a top New York restaurant where reservations were reputedly hard to get. To my surprise, the place was half empty that Friday night and there was no meteorological or urban disaster to explain it. I casually asked the maitre d', with whom I had a good relationship, about the situation.

"We got forty-three no-shows tonight," he replied in his thick French accent, "including the two eight-tops." (To those in The Life, there is a standard nomenclature of table sizes, with a table for two being a "deuce" and larger tables being "three-tops," "four-tops," etc.). Being a polite and formal guy, he was willing to leave it at that, but I pressed him to elaborate. He was clearly very upset about the problem and offered the following: "It's a disaster. All the ingredients are bought and many are perishable. The waiters all come in to work but now half of them we send home. And we plan so many special meals, like at the big table. But what can we do? We make everybody call to confirm. God forbid we overbook and somebody has to wait fifteen minutes. You should hear them complain! I buy them a drink and still they don't understand. But look around tonight. I think we are maybe the best restaurant in New York and this is what happens to us. We lose money on a night like this. You're a lawyer, no? Why can I not sue these forty-three people?"

Well, as a lawyer I can tell you that they can't win in court primarily because you haven't paid anything for the reservation. But as a human being I understand the frustration of restaurateurs surrounding this troublesome subject. If you book a room in a hotel and guarantee it with a credit card, then you pay for a night in that room whether you check in or not. If you fail to show up for a restaurant reservation, however, nothing happens to you. By some quirk of history, restaurants assume all the risk with respect to no-shows. Yet many consumers are radically insensitive to this situation: they book tables at five different restaurants and either no-show or last-minute cancel at four, they get annoyed when asked to confirm reservations and become furious when restaurants ask for a credit-card guarantee, and still they obstinately fail to understand why restaurants overbook or why there is sometimes a wait for a table. But from the restaurant's perspective, it's a matter of survival. If, despite a confirmation policy, a restaurant still gets no-shows in statistically predictable quantities (according to the *Chicago Tribune*, restaurants typically get between 10 and 40 percent no-shows), then the rational and necessary solutions are speculative overbooking and the occasional seating delays that result, or hard-and-fast credit-card guarantees for tables.

As diners, then, we have an obligation not to abuse our highly leveraged side of the reservations equation. By playing fair and demanding the same behavior of our friends, we can collectively reduce overbooking and waiting times. We should show up on time and cancel unneeded reservations as far in advance as possible. Even if you need to cancel an hour before the meal, the preferred course of action is to call. Some people are afraid to do this. They think they're going to get yelled at. In reality, I have never received anything but a polite response when canceling a reservation. What you will most likely hear is, "We appreciate your call." If you are going to be late, call as well. Most restaurants will be grateful for the knowledge. Anything is better than just not showing up.

There is a small movement toward credit-card-guaranteed restaurant reservations. If customers don't behave on the whole, this practice will become more widespread. Where etiquette fails, regulations are often needed.

I try to keep the overall dynamic of the reservations system in mind when, on occasion, I show up at a restaurant and my table isn't ready on time. To a certain extent, this is unavoidable. (Though if you reserve for early times you'll avoid this risk, because you'll be the first person to use your table that night.) But as a consumer you have certain reasonable expectations in such a situation. The host should provide you with an estimate of how long you'll need to wait and cordially offer you a seat at the bar. If the wait is longer than fifteen minutes for a confirmed reservation and you have arrived on time, at a high-quality restaurant the standard operating procedure should be to comp your drinks at the bar. Likewise, a customer should never be kept wondering. During prolonged waits, the staff should check in with you periodically to let you know the status of your table. If the wait is particularly long, say more than half an hour, there should be additional comps with the meal, such as dessert. While no customer is entitled to comps, good restaurants know this is the way to massage the overbooking situation to the satisfaction of everyone, and to generate repeat business by ending the meal on a high note.

Getting into a restaurant is nice, and for many consumers it's victory enough, but it's only the beginning. It's what happens to you in the restaurant that really counts. With awareness of how restaurants dole out the best tables, service, and even the best food, you can exercise a great degree of control over your dining experience.

On my second day with Isabel in the Eleven Madison Park reservations office, by which time I've sort of figured out through observation how the computer system works, curiosity gets the better of me: while Isabel and her assistant (sometimes she has as many as two assistants helping her take phone calls) are distracted, I type in my own name.

It seems I've dined at Eleven Madison Park on eight occasions, canceled one time, and have zero no-shows (thank goodness—that would have been embarrassing). My customer notes are alarmingly detailed, indicating various media outlets I write for, a list of journalism award nominations I've received, and a notation for a manager to "talk to chef" when I'm coming in. At the end of my customer notes there's a single word, "soigné."

"Soigné" (pronounced "swan-yay"), as used in The Life, refers to elegant, well-groomed service, derived from the French past participle of *soigner*, meaning "to take care of." It's a notation some restaurants use to designate clients who should receive extra care and attention: repeat customers, friends of the house, industry colleagues. Other restaurants might use notations like "VIP" or "lots of love," but most every restaurant has some variant—formal or informal—of the soigné system.

Every day at 4 P.M., Isabel prints up a reservation report for the evening, sorted by seating time and table size, with names and customer notes for each reservation. The computer also provides a summary of how many customers will be arriving every fifteen minutes throughout the evening.

On this afternoon, Isabel hands the list off to the anchor, Pauline Burer. The anchor is the air-traffic controller of the restaurant, responsible on her shift for maintaining an orderly house. Aided by other hosts, managers, and the service staff, Pauline makes sure the printed reservations report translates into dining-room reality.

She begins by highlighting all the large parties in pink—any group of five or more is considered a large table—and tentatively assigning tables so as to distribute the big groups throughout the restaurant's three dining areas. This also allows her to get a feel for when tables will be released and available for re-sitting: a party of eight dining early in the evening may be occupying two tables for four that can be used later. With a green highlighter, she marks any reservation with special customer notes—any birthdays, soigné notations, or special information.

Next, Pauline pulls out a stack of small triplicate forms that look like IOUs. These are the restaurant's "soigné chits." Pauline fills out a chit for each table that requires any special attention. The first one she writes up tonight is for a woman's sixty-fifth birthday. She carefully spells out the woman's name, fills in the table number and reservation time, and separates the forms. One copy will stay with her, one will go to the kitchen, and the other will get handed off to the server for that section of the dining room.

At 4:45 P.M., the restaurant's key managers and kitchen staff meet to go over the list. A manager will say a special hello to one table; another will get an extra dessert. Some customers have requested specific tables or servers in advance; tonight every one of those requests can be accommodated. Most of the time a restaurant will go out of its way to accommodate its most valued customers, and the most valued customers are the regulars and prospective regulars. As in any business, it's long-term repeat business—not the one-time hit—that keeps restaurants afloat.

Most every restaurant, then, is really two: the one the public eats at, and the one where the regulars dine. Being a regular affects every aspect of the dining experience, from getting that tough-to-book table on a busy Saturday night, to getting the waitstaff's best service, to getting special off-menu dishes and off-list wines. The best restaurant isn't the one with the highest Zagat rating, the most stars from the local paper, or that cute celebrity chef. It's the one where you're a regular.

This news can be discouraging to some, but it needn't be to you: by being a proactive and knowledgeable customer, you can start getting treated like a regular on your very first visit. A special relationship with a restaurant is one of life's great pleasures, and such a relationship can be far easier and quicker to establish than many people think. You don't need to be wealthy, a celebrity, or great-looking to be a regular. I'm none of the three, and I do pretty well in restaurants. And while you can't exactly become a regular in a single visit, you can make a lot of progress in that direction. The benefits of being a regular will, of course, increase with each visit to a restaurant.

Although each individual meal at a top restaurant should be excellent, most seasoned veteran diners take the long view. To them, eating a first meal at a restaurant is like a first date: it's a preview that helps you decide if you're going to want a second date. Most every restaurant, like every dating partner, keeps a little something in reserve for subsequent encounters. The first meal won't expose you to the full range of an establishment's capabilities, but it will give you a taste. On the later visits, things can get even more interesting.

But you can't make those repeat visits if you're constantly eating at the latest trendy place. Becoming a regular requires focus, whereas the relentless pursuit of the new and the different cuts directly against depth of enjoyment at just a few well-chosen places. There are more than six thousand restaurants in Chicago, and New York has something in the neighborhood of twenty-thousand; given how many close and open each week, any large city has too many to visit in a lifetime. Since you'll never visit them all, don't try. Instead, zero in on a handful of restaurants to satisfy your various dining needs—the special-occasion place, the business-lunch place, the neighborhood place where you go for a quick bite—and cultivate the heck out of your relationship with the staff at each one. You'll soon find you don't often get the urge to eat anywhere else, and that new restaurants have to fight to get onto your schedule instead of vice versa.

Before and during your first visit, do a little research. Every level of restaurant in every city has both an official and an unofficial dress code. The official dress code tells you the minimum ("no jeans, no sneakers" or "jackets required for gentlemen"), but what you want to know is the unofficial code: what are people really going to be wearing? The way to find out is to call ahead and ask. Other questions—there are no stupid ones—should be asked on the spot, while dining. Those in the service profession usually love to share their knowledge with newcomers to their restaurant or to fine dining in general. Whether you want to know what a funny-shaped utensil is for or what the best dish on the menu is, just look your server in the eye and ask, "Can you tell me about this?"

Most good restaurants' waitstaffs will recognize you after two or three visits. In that sense, anybody who visits a restaurant often enough eventually becomes a regular by default. But there are levels of regulars, and if you're going to visit the restaurant anyway, you may as well attain the highest, super-VIP level by being proactive. Learn the name of your waiter and the maitre d' or manager, and, more importantly, make certain they learn yours. The easiest way to accomplish this: "I really enjoyed my meal today. My name is Steven Shaw." If you aren't answered with, "Thank you, Mr. Shaw, my name is François, please let me know if there's anything I can do for you in the future," then there's something wrong with you, or with the restaurant. Of course you should use your name, not mine. There are still a few places out there that are annoyed with me for giving them bad reviews.

A restaurant is a business, but a relationship with a restaurant is not just about money. Especially when dealing with waitstaff, the human element can often eclipse financial concerns. Sure, money is important to people in the restaurant business, just as it's important to lawyers. But like the law, the restaurant business is a service business, and all lawyers know that there are good clients and bad clients, and that you can have bad billionaire clients and great penniless clients. When cultivating a relationship with a restaurant's service staff, being nice often counts at least as much as callously throwing money around. The use of "please" and "thank you," and general acknowledgment of your waiter as a fellow human being, will immeasurably improve your stock.

And there's something that counts as much or more than being nice: being interested. Any chef or waiter can tell you how disheartening it is to work so hard to create the best possible food and service experience, and then to dish it out to a mostly uncaring clientele that chose the restaurant for the scene, not the food. If you can distinguish yourself as someone who really cares about the restaurant's work, you will be everybody's favorite customer. The quickest approach? Again, ask questions, which indicates interest. Interest is one of the highest compliments you can pay. Of course, if you do choose to distribute a little extra cash, a twenty-dollar bill and a discreet "thank you" never hurts.

Do not, however, make the egregious mistake of faking it. Don't try to be someone you're not in order to impress a restaurant's staff. Aside from being undignified, this is doomed to failure. Every experienced waiter is a part-time amateur psychoanalyst and can spot a poseur clear across a crowded dining room. It's not necessary to try to appear learned about wine and food, or to appear absurdly enthusiastic. You'll get a lot further by deferring to the staff's expertise than you will by showing off your own. You may learn something, too.

So you're a regular at your favorite restaurant. Now what?

You could go on eating at the restaurant and just getting whatever special treatment the staff doles out to you. But that would be like buying a Porsche and never driving faster than 55 miles per hour. If you want to get the most out of your relationship with a restaurant, there's much more you can do.

Let's cut through all the disinformation and mythology here. Restaurants always hold back a few tables for their favored customers. Some say they don't, but they do. In countless restaurants I visited while researching this book, I looked at reservations books, either on paper or on computerized schedulers, and in every instance there were tables labeled "manager's slot" or "VIP hold" or "blocked." The random caller simply could not get those tables. If you visit a restaurant often, spend lots of money there, and are known to the staff, part of the restaurant's implicit promise to you is that you will always have access to a prime-time table on Saturday night.

But in order to take advantage of that situation, you need to identify yourself. If you're a regular at Eleven Madison Park and you call Isabel for a reservation, don't start by asking if there's a table available on Saturday night. Start by saying your name. As soon as you mention your name, she will be keying it into her computer, or she may just remember you. If the computer or the reservationist knows who you are, your chances of getting one of those blocked tables increase dramatically.

Some reservationists are better than others, or have more authority, so in the cases in which a reservationist can't help you what you need is the name and direct number of a key manager—or the chef or owner—who can put your name in the book even if the restaurant is ostensibly full. Furthermore, getting your favorite table and waiter should be a given.

As a regular, the ability to make special requests is also part of the deal. You want a multicourse tasting menu centered entirely around mushrooms, potatoes, or every part of a pig? You're bringing in a party of eight and you want to share in a whole roasted leg of lamb? You have a favorite cheese but it's not on the restaurant's cheese cart? You've got a special bottle of wine in your cellar and you want the chef to build a menu around it? Phone ahead and ask for what you want. Use your imagination. In the process of becoming a regular, chances are you've tasted everything on the restaurant's menu several times over. Being a regular means not being constrained by the same menu everyone else gets. Any good restaurant's staff will view a special request as an agreeable challenge. As long as your requests are reasonable and in keeping with the restaurant's style (and, presumably, you wouldn't have become a regular without this basic level of compatibility), you should be accommodated. As my friend Katie Loeb, the wine director at Rouge in Philadelphia, explains, the difference between a reasonable and an unreasonable request is the difference between "May I have that soft-shell crab sautéed instead of deep fried?" and "I'd like the seven grain bread with no oats, please."

There are few things more comforting in life than hearing a waiter say, "The usual?" Be it a particular cocktail, an appetizer the kitchen prepares only for you, or extra salt in your butter, your rituals should be remembered and honored. Specifically in the business-entertaining context, there are a number of things you can do to coordinate with the restaurant. Do you always pay the bill? Then set up a house account. The restaurant will keep an imprint of your credit card on file, and you can leave standing instructions to add an 18 percent gratuity. Do you always need to conclude a business lunch in exactly seventy-five minutes? A good restaurant can make that happen.

Restaurants can also sometimes get you reservations at other restaurants. The clique of top restaurants in any city, and across the country, is like OPEC, and the servers, managers, and kitchen staff all know one another and have been trading off jobs for ages. If you're a regular at restaurant A, and you want to go to restaurant B where you've never been, chances are somebody at restaurant A has a strong contact, a wife, a brother, or a lover working at restaurant B. Have somebody make a phone call on your behalf. Remember, that person over at restaurant B probably has customers that want to come to restaurant A. It's all about reciprocity.

The elite-restaurant cartel phenomenon extends across the country and around the globe. When you head to the other coast or overseas, especially if the goal is gastronomic tourism, your favorite restaurant becomes a pseudo-travel agency. If you're planning to visit a Michelin three-star restaurant in France, you may have better luck getting a reservation if the chef or maitre d' at your favorite restaurant makes it for you. I've had chefs in France ask me to hand-carry letters back to their chef friends in America who made reservations on my behalf. I've got to think those same chefs paid a little extra attention to my meals. Nor does the menu of travel planning services end there. For example, fine restaurants buy a lot of wine and the larger wine producers and distributors are very aggressive marketers. If you're going to be in Burgundy, find out with which producers the restaurant has a relationship. Even if the restaurant has no direct contacts in the region, there should be an importer or distributor who can exercise some pull on your behalf. This little bit of entrée makes all the difference. You will be assured a VIP winery tour and tasting unattainable by ordinary tourists. One call from Joseph Nase, the beverage director at the old Lespinasse, was all it took to get me a private tour of Louis Latour's vineyards and chateau, including a private tasting in the nineteenth century cellar of Chateau Corton Grancey.

Remember, though, once you're part of a restaurant's family, you have certain obligations. In many ways, regulars are more restricted in their actions than strangers. As a regular, you're under an increased obligation to be courteous, to be understanding, and to be discreet. Part of the bargain is that you can't go around telling everybody else about the special treatment you receive, because it will interfere with their enjoyment of the restaurant if they go—VIP treatment is a secret bargain. And it should be understood that the special relationship is between the restaurant and you alone. Don't overstep the bounds of the relationship by demanding reservations or special treatment for your friends. If you do want the restaurant to know someone is under your umbrella of political capital, there's an easy way to do it: "My friends are coming in tonight and I'd like to buy them a bottle of Champagne." They'll get the idea.

At 4:50 P.M., "family meal" (this is what those in The Life call the staff meal) is served at Eleven Madison Park. A buffet line is set up in the kitchen and a section of the dining room is cleared for the staff. Selections include penne in a vodka sauce, sliced flank steak, vegetarian lasagna, a green salad, a chopped tomato salad, steamed carrots, and roasted new potatoes. The night I share in family meal, I try a little bit (okay, a lot) of everything, and make a note to ask for the lasagna recipe.

By the time the staffers collect their meals, pour themselves drinks from the soda fountain, and sit down, the 4:45 P.M. management meeting is wrapping up and the managers have a few minutes to brief the waitstaff on the key elements of the evening's game plan. This is also the opportunity to discuss general administration. Today a few servers have underperformed on their menu tests (servers at Eleven Madison Park and many other top restaurants take a periodic written test in order to answer questions like "Can the chicken be made without butter?" and "Which entrees contain nuts?") and will need to re-take them the following week.

Next, two of the sous-chefs (literally "under" chefs—these are the lieutenants who keep the kitchen brigade functioning day-in day-out) bring out sample plates of the evening's special: roasted lamb with two types of wild mushrooms. The sous-chefs explain the dish and then cut it up into bite-size pieces so each server can have a taste. Servers are encouraged to give feedback on the dish, because the cooks know that if the servers don't like a dish they won't try to sell it to their customers. This one seems like a winner. It's time for the dinner service.

In 2004, Eleven Madison Park received the James Beard Foundation Award for Outstanding Service. It's a good thing these awards can't be revoked, because tonight the restaurant has just added the world's worst employee to its service team: me.

When I started researching the behind-the-scenes world of restaurants, I figured it would be a simple matter to get on the floor at a top New York place. It wasn't. Thanks to pudgy hands and an ill-defined center of gravity, the first time I attempted to carry two plates without leaving thumbprints on them (in proper restaurant service, you grip plates with the fold of the palm of your hand, not with your thumb) I dropped them both—two pieces of Bernardaud Limoges china down the drain. On account of nearsightedness and astigmatism, I can't quite get the pouring-water-and-wine thing right, so I'm as likely as not to pour on the far side of the glass. (At home, I touch the tip of the bottle or the spout of the pitcher to the edge of the glass—a no-no in restaurant service.) And on account of being, shall we say, big boned I need a double-XL uniform, something that isn't typically kept on hand at most restaurants.

The compromise: I won't handle any food or wear a server's uniform. Rather, my cover will be that of an assistant manager. (The managers wear conservative business suits rather than staff uniforms.) It is everybody's sincerest hope that no customer tries to flag me down for a special request, and that I don't precipitate any major spillage, collisions, or breakage. To add to the risk and already palpable tension, tonight is Saturday night of Memorial Day weekend.

The night I spend on the floor, my unlucky supervisor is Alex Jarman. A compact, blond Memphis native, she looks sharp in her black suit and blue steel eyeglasses. Standing next to her at approximately three times her size and weight, I look and feel ungainly and out of place. Alex is tonight's anchor.

At 5:30 P.M., the first customers start to arrive at the podium. Alex and I are there to greet them. At 5:31 P.M., my plan to smile and remain silent while Alex does the talking collapses when a guest asks me what kind of flowers are in the arrangement by the front door. "Forsythia," I say proudly, remembering a staff meeting. After the guests are seated, Alex whispers, "The forsythia were yesterday. These are lilacs." Of course, forsythia and lilacs don't remotely alike.

When they arrive at their tables, the customers are presented with menus and wine lists. Later there will be dessert menus. This is actually a light informational load by the standards of some restaurants. There are places where you're presented with so much paperwork you'd be forgiven for thinking you're at a real estate closing. There may be a regular dinner menu, a preset chef's multicourse tasting menu or two, a specials list either spoken or written, a wine list, a dessert menu, and perhaps even a dessert wine and liqueur list. How is one to make sense of all these documents?

There's no way to become a food or wine expert overnight, or even in a year. But you don't need expertise. All you need is enough confidence to ask questions. The rest is up to the restaurant. In hiring staff, training them, and holding all those meetings every day, a top restaurant has taken on the burden of providing expertise. If you provide an opening by asking a question, any good restaurant's staff should be more than happy to share that expertise with you.

One of the most basic lines of inquiry, which can lead to a highly productive dialogue, is asking servers what their favorite dishes are, and what dishes the chef considers specialties of the house. While your tastes may vary from the norm, and while you shouldn't order bass if you hate bass, the recommendations of waitstaff at good restaurants are valuable indicators of what the chef, staff, and customers tend to enjoy.

If you're an adventurous omnivore, at many top restaurants you may be able to opt for a tasting menu, also sometimes called a menu *degustation*. With a tasting menu, you trade choice for variety. Instead of an appetizer, entree, and dessert, a tasting menu may present you with five, seven, or in some restaurants, like Rocco DiSpirito's now-defunct Union Pacific, as many as twenty-one smaller courses. Many people love tasting menus and order them whenever available. Others prefer to choose and to eat just a few larger dishes. People on both sides will emphatically inform you that they're right. Try some of each and see what works for you, and bear in mind that some restaurants may excel at tasting menus while others may not.

Daily specials are another issue over which people have strongly divided opinions. As with tasting menus, I tend to approach these restaurant by restaurant. At a top-drawer establishment like Eleven Madison Park, specials tend to be just what they say they are: special. At lesser restaurants, they may just be repackaged versions of the regular menu dishes but at a higher price, or, worse, overstocked ingredients that are getting old. If I trust a restaurant in general, I trust the restaurant's specials. If there's any uncertainty, I stick to the regular menu. In any event, if the prices of specials are not printed or recited, you should never hesitate to ask.

One of the most daunting parts of ordering, especially for those who are new to fine dining but even for many seasoned veterans, is the selection of wine. A significant restaurant with an ambitious wine program might have more than a thousand wine choices on its list. Even a casual brasserie or bistro is likely to have more choices than you could possibly read through without freezing out everybody else at your table and winning yourself a "wine geek" label or worse.

In better restaurants, then, it always pays to seek assistance from the sommelier, or wine steward. The sommelier's role is to know the restaurant's wine and food offerings better than any customer possibly could. Even other professional sommeliers seek the advice of the sommelier when dining out.

A sommelier will most likely make a sensible wine recommendation, provided you participate in the decision. Your part of the bargain, then, is to make your needs and preferences known. If you haven't yet ordered, you'll benefit from telling the sommelier what you plan to eat. Any preferences you can articulate, from the most basic "I like my wines on the sweeter side" to more technical statements of regional and stylistic preference, will help the sommelier narrow the field. Most importantly, there is the matter of price. Once you've decided how much your budget is for a bottle of wine, the best way to communicate this to the sommelier is to point to any bottle on the list at your comfortable price and say, "Something in this range, please."

The wine service ritual is romantic and entertaining, but it's mostly pragmatic. The main goal is to determine whether or not the wine is "corked." It's a reality of the wine world that as many as one in ten bottles will be corked, meaning they will be tainted by a foul-smelling and -tasting mold that grows in corks. (It has nothing to do, as some mistakenly think, with bits of cork in the bottle, which would be harmless.) To me, it smells like feet. If your nose detects such an off aroma when you smell or taste the wine the sommelier or server has poured, send the bottle back. If you're not sure, ask the sommelier for confirmation—restaurants usually get credit from their distributors for corked bottles, so they tend not to mind taking them back, and even if they did mind, it wouldn't be your problem. The wine service ritual is not, however, intended for you to see if you like the wine. If the wine is damaged, send it back. If it's simply not the exact wine you wished you'd ordered, mention this to the sommelier, but be prepared to drink it and chalk it up to experience unless the sommelier offers a replacement.

It's not always necessary to order bottles of wine, however. Sometimes, if you're a couple and don't drink very much, or you're ordering very different dishes, you may want to inquire about wines by the glass, or at some restaurant, by the quartino (a 250 ml mini-carafe that's enough for two small glasses) or half-bottle (375 ml).

Plenty of restaurants, unfortunately, don't have a sommelier or even any server or manager who knows much about wine. This is your cue that you shouldn't be spending much money on wine at the restaurant. Instead, order something inexpensive and safe, if anything at all. Know the names of a few of the major producers of reliable red and white wines—information you can get by reading a couple of issues of *Wine Spectator* (which includes a pullout reference card with every issue) or surfing the Web—for such contingencies. Or do without, and use the money for a better bottle of wine later on, at a better restaurant.

Under no circumstances, however, should you ever feel compelled to order wine in any restaurant. Aside from whatever fixed price menu or per-customer minimum a restaurant reveals in writing on the menu, everything else is optional. You are entirely within your rights and the scope of appropriate conduct as a customer to drink tap water, order food only, and skip coffee. A server should always ask if you want these things (at most restaurants it's a requirement of the job and servers will get in trouble if they don't do it), but should never aggressively try to upsell you on anything. If that happens, just smile knowingly and say, "No, thank you."

Back at Eleven Madison Park, as my feet and lower back are becoming sore from standing in one place at the podium, I reflect on the sheer physicality of working at a restaurant. As a lifelong desk worker, I've always had the luxury of sitting down, going to the restroom when I need to, and taking meals and sleep when needed. In my home office, I have the additional option of being slovenly. Restaurant employees, by contrast, spend their professional lives on their feet, they need to pay attention to their hygiene and bearing, and they dine, sleep, and vacation at odd hours. I couldn't do it.

Nor could I ever bluff as well as Alex does when an unexpected super-VIP customer arrives without a reservation, thinking he has one. His reservation had actually been for the night before—he was recorded as a no-show—but there he is, and the restaurant is nearly full. In one of the greatest exhibitions of nonchalance I've ever seen, Alex shows him to his favorite table, number 64, as though everything is normal. She then scurries back to the podium to make adjustments to the seating plan. The computer is showing a couple of tables eating dessert (the tables change color on Alex's screen as the servers indicate on their computer substations—all of which are networked together—where each table is in the progression of its meal). "Maybe someone will finish early, and someone else will be late," she hopes. More likely, someone will need to wait a few minutes for a table.

Any restaurant, no matter how good, gets its fair share of complaints, some justified and some not. A good managerial staff like the one at Eleven Madison Park heads off most complaints at the pass by watching the tables and the waitstaff. But a few things slip through the cracks. A customer waits too long for wine, and gets his food before the bottle of wine arrives. Someone else is served the wrong dish. In the grand scheme of things, serving hundreds of customers a night, a couple of errors is an excellent record. But to those customers the mistakes can put a serious damper on the evening.

That's why if something goes wrong in a restaurant it's important to speak up. Servers, managers, and chefs are human. They make mistakes, they get distracted, they have personal problems, and are besieged by all the other little difficulties of the human condition. Most of the time, though, when their mistakes are pointed out to them, they want to make things right. And if they don't, there's always a manager or an owner above them who will.

What a restaurant's staff can't do is read your mind. I know many people are uncomfortable speaking up in restaurants, either because they're intimidated by the staff or because they don't want to put on a big show in front of the other people at the table. Some of us have families that raised us not to complain, but the restaurant context isn't the place to live that way. In restaurants, it's best for everybody if you make your complaint known as soon as you become aware of a problem. If you prefer to complain privately, excuse yourself from the table as though you're going to the bathroom and pull a manager aside on your way: "I just wanted to let you know that every time I need water refilled I have to search and wave for several minutes to get it. I'm trying to have a celebratory dinner here and this is putting a damper on my evening. Do you think you can help?" At any good restaurant, it is virtually guaranteed that the manager will not only address the issue right away with the service staff, but also will pay extra special attention to your table for the rest of the evening. If not, don't return to the restaurant.

Speaking up is one of the keys to getting what you want. If you're being shown to a table that you don't like, for example one next to a noisy group or a bathroom entrance, request a different table before you sit down. Even if there are no other available tables, say you'll be willing to wait. A few minutes of awkwardness at the outset is better than a few hours at a table you won't enjoy. If a dish is overcooked or otherwise deficient, send it back and say why. If you feel the pace of your meal is rushed, ask to have it slowed down. If your server or a manager asks "Is everything okay?" and it isn't, don't say it is. Review your bill carefully, because if you notice an error the next day it will be infinitely more difficult to correct. So long as you are civil when voicing reasonable complaints, you are in the right.

Writing a follow-up letter of complaint is another way to convey your dissatisfaction, but by then it's too late for the restaurant to fix the problem. I prefer to make complaints immediately, no matter how uncomfortable it makes me, so as to fix the meal before it becomes a bad memory. I reserve follow-up letters for the complaints that weren't fixed, even after being voiced.

At the end of the dinner shift, when the last customers finish their dessert and coffee at around 12:30 A.M., I look over a few of the checks. Eleven Madison Park is not a cheap restaurant. Cocktails, wine, three courses, and coffee can easily cost $100 or more per person, and that's nowhere near the upper limit of top restaurant prices. At the Japanese restaurant Masa, probably the most expensive restaurant in America right now, the minimum dinner price is $300 per person.

There are plenty of people who can't abide the notion of spending $100 per person on dinner when they can get a wholesome, nutritious, and often good-tasting meal at the local diner for around $10, or cook one at home for a third of that cost. Dining, as opposed to eating, is a luxury. So are many other things. You never need to go to a baseball game; you can watch it on TV for free. You never need to buy nice clothes; you can wear hand-me-downs. You don't need a Mercedes or even a Toyota; depending on where you live you can drive a Kia, take the bus, ride a bicycle, or even walk. You don't need a house or a big apartment; you can live in the smallest possible digs. For better or worse, that's not how most of us conduct ourselves. We have our luxuries and our indulgences, and for those who love to dine one of our indulgences is restaurants.

But there's no need to waste money in restaurants. Getting what you want entails getting the most out of your dining dollar. Through careful management of the check you can enjoy more meals for the same amount of money. For me, that means never ordering bottled water (often $6 or more per bottle at fine restaurants), skipping coffee, and keeping to a tight wine budget. For others, it could mean never ordering wine at all. The important thing is to be aware of what you're spending so you only spend what you want to spend. One reason restaurants love those six- and eight-tops is that in large groups self-restraint tends to break down and the bar tab in particular can be astronomical. You can limit this group dynamic by agreeing with your party in advance what the limits on ordering or the division of the bill will be. It may feel a little bit awkward to monitor expenditures and especially to discuss them with others, but at the end of the night when the bill comes you'll all feel a lot better than you otherwise would have.

Most restaurants offer ways of trying their food on a budget. Lunch menus, pretheater specials, and seasonal promotions are great ways to test a kitchen's mettle without a major economic commitment. Often the food you get on these cheaper menus is exactly what you'd get on the full-price dinner menu, except you have fewer choices and sometimes the portions are smaller. Becoming a regular at a restaurant can also be a good investment, because once you establish the relationship you may see the occasional comped dish arrive at your table.

Price, however, is not the measure of value. True value is about getting what you pay for, and sometimes there's better value in saving up for one splurge meal at a truly excellent restaurant than in having three meals at middle-of-the-road establishments that offer nothing special. What I hope to show you throughout this book is what differentiates the special from the run-of-the-mill.

Before they can leave for the night, a couple of exhausted members of the Eleven Madison Park waitstaff have the job of dividing up the tips. The tip you leave on the table, in most restaurants, goes into a pool. Every member of the service team, from the captains and waiters to the bussers and bartenders, has a certain number of "points" in the pool for that shift. The pool is divided by the total number of points and distributed. These days, with credit cards the most popular form of payment and the IRS focusing on restaurant staff, the tips are usually recorded in a computer and taxes withheld on paychecks.

And then the restaurant's employees eat their dinner. Most people I know in The Life eat three meals a day. The first, they call breakfast. This is known as lunch or an early-afternoon snack to us civilians and typically consists of coffee, a sandwich or leftovers, and more coffee. The second is family meal, though it often extends through the dinner service with catch-as-catch-can charred ends of roasted meat, buttered rolls, excess desserts doled out by the kitchen's pastry assistants, and more coffee. Meal number three—the one most recognizable as an actual human dining ritual—commences late at night, the official feeding hour of those who live The Life, especially in the 24-hour economies of the larger urban centers.

If there is an official food of those in The Life, it has got to be sushi. A private eye tasked with locating a restaurant staffer after closing time would do well to canvass every sushi bar that's open late. If you talk to most any group of restaurant workers—both waitstaff and cooks—you will find a high level of sushi consumption. I think this is because, at some point, those in the food business—the Western part of that business, at least—become overly saturated with flavor and sensory information. They get sick of looking at plates composed of meat, sauce, veg, and starch. Japanese cuisine, in its minimalism, is a refreshing antidote to that chronic overstimulation: it activates a different set of receptors and acts as a short vacation.

Most restaurants above the level of fast-food and take-out joints, even those that serve some of the lesser-known regional cuisines of Asia or South America, are organized the same way: you sit at a table, you get a menu, you order from a server, and the server brings your food. At a sushi bar, unlike in most restaurants, you interact directly with a chef. The chef is your server. One's knowledge of how to interact with waitstaff thus carries over to a great degree at a sushi bar. But Japanese restaurants have many of their own rules, so it's helpful to examine for a few moments the subject of sushi bar etiquette, because it is a special case where getting what you want requires a unique strategy. (The sushi bar style is also starting to be emulated in non-sushi restaurants, such as at Joel Robuchon's Atelier in Paris and the ChikaLicious dessert restaurant in New York—Western restaurants where customers sit at counters and order directly from chefs.)

One thing I learned as a lawyer at a big commercial firm was how to look as though I knew what I was doing, even when I didn't. That skill is particularly valuable at sushi bars, because getting the best meal at a sushi bar is all about attitude. Speaking Japanese, of course, helps. Being Japanese is even better, though you don't want to be Japanese and not speak Japanese, because that combination sends you all the way to the bottom of the sushi bar hierarchy. In any event, I'm none of the above, so swagger is the only tool available to me. Here's my strategy for extracting the best possible meal.

For starters, you have to be at the sushi bar. There are two types of people eating sushi at a Japanese restaurant: those at the sushi bar, and the tourists. The only way someone at a regular table gets access to the best and most complete selection of sushi the restaurant has to offer is by being favored by one of the sushi chefs. To cultivate such a relationship, go for an early dinner, before things get busy, so you can command maximum individual attention. Preferably, you should go alone or with one cooperative confederate, because your first meal at any given sushi bar is serious business. Bring lots of money.

When you get to the sushi bar, make eye contact with the nearest sushi chef. Give him (or, in extremely rare instances, her) a quick nod. Try to say with your eyes, "Very serious sushi customer coming your way, chef." Don't try to bow unless you've got proper bowing training, because if you bow too much or too little, you and the chef will get caught in an endless loop of reciprocal bowing and you'll never get any food.

Without being rude, you need to dismiss the waitstaff almost completely. Refuse a menu. Say you're ordering sushi by the piece, and that you're ordering it directly from the chef. Let the waiter bring you some water, some tea, or a beer, but don't let anybody come between you and the sushi chef.

Announce that you'll be starting with sashimi. Say it as though you know it's obvious that anybody with a clue would start with sashimi. Order two pieces of sashimi: one piece of regular tuna and one piece of toro (belly) tuna. Some places have more than one level of toro, in which case you should get the fattiest available. Do not place the rest of your order. Just get those pieces. When they're placed in front of you, eye them very carefully. Look as though you know exactly how to evaluate a piece of sashimi. Pick it up with chopsticks, hold it up, check it out from all angles. Give it some thought. Then eat it, without any soy sauce or wasabi (or, at most, just a tiny bit of each). Reflect deeply as you chew. If you've done your job right, the sushi chef will be extremely interested to know whether you approved of your tuna. If you did like it, this is the time for a knowing smile. If, however, you think your tuna was lousy, it's time to close the books, cut your losses, pay, and leave. Rest assured, these days, there are most likely many other sushi bars within a short distance.

The ability to judge a piece of tuna comes primarily from experience, but the main things you're looking for are a clean taste (which is often described as "fresh," even though the freshest tuna you'll get at even the best sushi restaurant is probably a few days old—don't worry, it will taste fabulous if it's good tuna that has been properly iced), a buttery and fleshy (not mealy) texture, and, in the case of the toro, a texture even softer than butter—more like the silken texture of lard. You also want an absence of off-smelling ("fishy") odors, and you want the sushi chef's knife technique to be outstanding—if you can cut a nicer piece of fish yourself, it means the chef is either lazy or incompetent.

If you approve the tuna, order additional sashimi. Remember, fish isn't a fungible commodity like frozen orange juice. Even at the best sushi restaurant, not every piece of fish will be at its best every day. Luckily, the sushi chef knows exactly what is best on any given day. So this is the time to ask questions and get advice, and to follow said advice.

At an appropriate break in the action, announce, "Now, sushi." This will transition you from the naked raw slices of sashimi to the crosswise slices of the same fish mounted on little lumps of sweetened vinegared rice, or rolled with rice in a seaweed (nori) wrapper. I like to start with tuna and toro again here, in order to see the changes they undergo when made into sushi. The warmth of the rice and the different cutting technique used for sushi (nigiri sushi is the technical term for the individual pieces, as opposed to the other major category, maki, aka sushi rolls) combine to give a completely different experience of the exact same food. Also note whether the rice has a little bit of a vinegar taste and a bit of sweetness. It should, but not too much. Proceed to follow the sushi chef's recommendations. Then finish up with a sushi roll or two. Try not to embarrass yourself by getting a California roll. Go for toro-and-scallion, or again solicit some suggestions. Skip dessert, request the check, pay the check (which will be staggering), and tip a normal amount.

If you've decided that this sushi chef is someone you want to work with and learn from (this is like choosing a psychoanalyst), ask the sushi chef his name, tell him yours (or earnestly present a business card with both hands), and give him twenty bucks (unless he's the owner, in which case no tip is necessary). Go back soon to reinforce his memory of you, but this time allow him to choose all your fish (the procedure known as *omakase*).

Now you have your very own personal sushi chef, and there's no reason ever to go to any other sushi restaurant unless he gets a new job (in which case, your loyalty is to the sushi chef, not the establishment). Now you're ready to take dates, friends, and business associates—even Japanese-speaking Japanese ones—out for sushi.

As this civilian rides home on the subway at 4:00 A.M. after a late-night encounter with The Life—in this case I've joined a group of cooks and servers at two different restaurants and a bar—I recall my earliest fine-dining meals and the feeling of helplessness and confusion I sometimes had. What to wear? What wine to order? What to do if they try to seat me at the crummy table near the men's room door?

This book is, in part, my answer to all those questions. I try to address many of the most commonly asked fine-dining newbie questions and concerns specifically, but in the final analysis you can resolve most situations yourself by keeping an open mind and observing three basic rules: If you don't know, ask. If you don't get the treatment you deserve, complain. And always say please and thank you.

CHAPTER TWO

Behind the Kitchen Door, and Beyond

"You call that a brunoise?" Matt Seeber, sous-chef at one of New York's top restaurants, Gramercy Tavern, has had the misfortune of being placed in charge of me for the next week. With a flick of the wrist, my personal drill sergeant casts my last half-hour's work in the garbage. "If the chef saw your sorry excuse for a brunoise, he'd send you packing." He unholsters a 10-inch chef's knife. "Good thing celery is cheap," he growls, "I'll show you again." In a blur of activity, Matt hones his knife on a steel, splits a celery stalk down the middle, lays the halves on the cutting board, trims them into rectangles and, moving his knife in smooth horizontal strokes, shaves each rectangle into 1/16-inch slivers. He then dices each sliver into identical 1/16-inch cubes. It takes him five minutes to parse one celery stalk—about 4,096 cubes, by my computation. This is the dreaded brunoise (pronounced "broon-WAHZ"), which will be the bane of my existence in the days to come.

"Got it? Okay, I need about a quart. Then you can do the carrots."

Three hours later, I move on to peeling several hundred boiled fingerling potatoes with a paring knife. The potatoes are still hot, and they scald my fingers as I try to hold them—but they are impossible to peel cold. Then I prepare the bayaldi, a huge baking sheet of razor-thin, alternating one-inch circles of zucchini, yellow squash, eggplant, and tomato laid over caramelized onions. My feet are getting sore from standing on the hard, slippery tile floor (even though I wore what I thought were my most comfortable shoes) and my back is aching from bending over the counter—and it's only my first day. Now it's time to make dinner.

At 5:30 P.M., as Gramercy Tavern's first customers are seated, Tom Colicchio, Executive Chef, takes his post on "the pass," a worktable at the front of the kitchen where every dish passes before his eyes and receives its final garnish before being dispatched to the dining room. One of the floor managers sticks her head into the kitchen. "Nineteen menus," she says, indicating how many customers are seated and studying their options. In the dining room, the section captains are answering questions, taking orders and passing the handwritten order slips off to their waiters, who enter them into a computer.

As the table receives the evening's amuse bouche, the little Micros printer on the pass comes to life and spits out the first order of the evening. (Most restaurants today use these computerized ordering systems called POS—or Point of Sale—systems, from Micros and other companies.) Chef Tom snatches the ticket and calls out the appetizers for table 235: "Ordering one partridge, one tartare, two green salad, one urchin." The kitchen springs to life. Jonathan, the steely-eyed line cook in charge of partridge, foie gras, and a few other meat dishes, begins the appetizer—two boneless cylinders of partridge breast wrapped in cabbage and served with a consommé. At the same time, Juliet, at the shellfish station, starts to heat the sea urchin fondue and mashed potato mixture, while Hector, at the garde manger ("gahrd mahn-ZHAY," where cold food is prepared) station, takes a portion of tuna tartare with cucumber vinaigrette out of the fridge (leaving it in its steel mold) and prepares to toss two green salads.

When the hot dishes are almost finished, the chef calls "finish tartare, salads," at which point Hector unmolds the tuna and plates the salads. Chef Tom garnishes the partridge with coarse salt and fresh marjoram and sprinkles the urchin (served in its shell) with chopped chives. With a final command of "pick up!" three runners grab the orders (quickly glancing at a copy of the order ticket to see which guest gets which dish, and in what sequence—the ticket even indicates, by a "W," which guests are female) and deliver them to the dining room. With a red pencil, Chef Tom notes the time the appetizers went out. The meat entrees are already cooking, and the fish will get started in a couple of minutes.

The first order of partridge gets sent back. "What's the matter with it?" Chef Tom asks the captain. "She says it's not what she expected," he replies. (This is, incidentally, the first night of the Autumn menu, and almost every dish is new.) Everybody in the kitchen has tasted this partridge dish and the consensus of these professional cooks (and me) is that it's great. Chef Tom sighs. "It's going to be a long night." The partridge order is replaced with a salad of cured hamachi.

Meanwhile, other orders are pouring in. Within an hour, Juliet is "in the weeds" (swamped) because twenty-three customers have spontaneously and simultaneously ordered lobster in the past few minutes—and the red meat station is inundated with orders for "beef, MR" and "lamb, MR." Chef Tom relinquishes the pass to Matt and ambles over to assist Juliet (this kind of thing, which happens every day, doesn't constitute a crisis in Tom's world). He looks at the twenty-three spice-rubbed lobsters waiting to be sautéed. "We need more skillets."

"What do you mean they're not ready?" Matt says to a waiter, as he stares down at two plates of monkfish ("monk" in kitchen-speak) destined for table 245. "She's got one bite left of her app and they're just staring at each other, all starry-eyed," reports the waiter. Matt puts the two plates aside and turns to me. "Looks like we're having monk for dinner." He surveys the accumulated order tickets and sees that table 220 has two monkfish orders in the works. "Eric, how long on those other two monk?" "About five." "Okay, fire two more—four all day. Make those first two real nice for the starry-eyed lovers." 245 gets 220's monk and 220, which was ahead of schedule anyway, suffers only about a one-minute delay.

By 11:30 P.M., when things finally quiet down, the kitchen has served three or more courses each to over 240 guests. But even as the exhausted line cooks clean their stations and Matt wraps the little printer in cellophane (to keep it dry), there is still plenty to be done over at the pastry station. Christina and Connie—two of the assistant pastry chefs—will be baking apple tarts and lemon soufflés to order for at least another hour, and they'll be cleaning their station until 1:30 A.M. The head pastry chef will be in at about 5 A.M. to start the next day's desserts.

For a midnight snack, I have a big plate of leftover mashed potatoes (perhaps the most rewarding part of working in a restaurant kitchen is the virtually unlimited opportunity for snacking—this is basically my idea of heaven), plus a glass of Bruno Paillard Champagne and two Advil.

Modesto is Gramercy Tavern's produce buyer. I don't know if that's his first or last name—everybody just calls him Modesto. A visit to the Union Square Greenmarket with Modesto is like a trip to Disneyland with Mickey Mouse as your tour guide. Modesto is King of the Greenmarket. After four hours of sleep, I meet Modesto at the restaurant's loading dock at 7 A.M. Today, I'm trying a different footwear strategy: Timberland light hiking boots and Thor-Lo socks. We grab two hand trucks and walk the three-and-a-half blocks to the Greenmarket—just long enough for me to realize that my boots are going to be a complete failure.

Modesto is a big guy, but he moves like a water bug. I scramble to keep up as we approach the first stalls. Modesto sees a pile of leeks and he's off like a shot. He picks up a bunch, sniffs them, squeezes them and holds them three inches from his eyes. "Nice," he rules. "How many you got?" he asks the woman behind the table. "About fifty pounds, Modesto." (Everybody knows Modesto by name.) "Okay," says Modesto, turning away (apparently, this indicates that he wants to buy them all).

"How about some yellow tomatoes?" the woman calls out, but Modesto is already two stalls down, tasting radish sprouts. I've lost all track of time working in the kitchen, and it's not until I see Modesto talking to two farmers dressed as cows that I realize it's Halloween. One of the cows conspiratorially hands Modesto a small envelope of tomato seeds. "I send these seeds back to my family in my country," confesses Modesto. "I hope they grow there." But every time I try to ask Modesto where his country is, he's gone.

At the Paffenroth Gardens stand, where Modesto makes his largest purchase of the day (about three hundred pounds of assorted herbs and vegetables), Alex Paffenroth has hot homemade tamales waiting for me and Modesto in the back of his truck. "Just one each?" Modesto accuses the burly, silver-bearded Paffenroth. "Yeah, just one—you're getting too fat and," gesturing toward me, "the gringo don't look like he's starving either. Now get on out of here so we can pack up your stuff." Modesto and Paffenroth exchange hugs and bone-jarring pats on the back, and we're off.

In season, Gramercy Tavern gets most of its produce at the Union Square Greenmarket (during the winter months, the restaurant works with commercial produce distributors). This reliance on small farms can lead to some interesting situations in the kitchen of the "What am I supposed to do with all this salsify?" variety, but Tom Colicchio is a fanatic when it comes to fresh, seasonal produce. In keeping with this spirit of unpredictability, Modesto makes his purchases without any sort of shopping list. He doesn't even have a pencil. I ask, "Modesto, how the heck do you know what to buy?" He holds up four fingers and explains, "Four years! Four years I do this! I know what to buy."

At the end of our tour, we circle around to pick up Modesto's orders. Nearly every farmer has an apple, a muffin, or some other treat waiting for us—all of which we consume with great relish. It takes two men six trips each to get the produce back to the restaurant.

Modesto deftly maneuvers his cart around every crack in the sidewalk, while I keep getting stuck. As I collapse in a chair back at the restaurant, Modesto taunts, "This is nothing! In summer, I do this all day."

It's Marathon Sunday, and a group of twenty Australian runners is having a dinner party in Gramercy Tavern's private dining room. Now I'm wearing running sneakers.

Gramercy Tavern maintains a separate area of the kitchen that services only the private dining room, which can accommodate up to twenty-four guests. That way, when it's time to make twenty-four lobsters, the rest of the kitchen doesn't grind to a halt. On this night, Matt and I are assigned to cook for the party (or, rather, Matt will cook and I'll try not to chop my fingers off). But first I have to make the brunoise.

At least half of what goes on in a restaurant kitchen is prep work, and it's dizzyingly boring. I've got the brunoise job down to about two hours now (fifteen minutes or so is the goal for a real professional cook), but there's plenty more to do. I spend almost an hour arranging tiny, over-lapping, paper-thin slices of potato on gigantic cookie sheets (this is similar to the bayaldi I made the other day, so for all intents and purposes I'm a seasoned veteran). In the end, these potato shingles get cut up into small rect-angles and used as a garnish. You can barely even see it on the plate because it's partially concealed by a piece of bass. But none of this vegetable work is nearly as rough as the afternoon when Matt foisted me off on one of the prep cooks in the basement and I butchered and tied two dozen loins of lamb, the same number of rabbits, and several quail.

Gramercy Tavern is known for unpretentious American cuisine with little elaborate preparation, yet most dishes require about ten elements when plated. If you look at one of the simplest—a piece of sirloin with mashed potatoes (potato puree, actually)—it seems pretty basic. But on the plate you have a dollop of sauce (which took all day to make) hidden under the steak; a ring of potato puree around that; a couple of sliced fingerling potatoes on the side; some sautéed sprouts on top of the steak; two pieces of braised leek (a real hassle—leeks are very difficult to clean); a little pile containing two pieces of salsify and one slice of black truffle; another little pile of lentils and pearl onions; and multiple fresh herbs and coarse salt sprinkled on the various components of the dish (not to mention the various stocks and seasonings needed to braise the leeks, cook the lentils, etc.).

The separate private party facility has an unanticipated benefit, which is that it's a great place for a beginner like me to observe. Because the private-party cook knows in ad-vance exactly what he will be making (private party menus are usually preset or limited to a couple of choices), he can prep and cook everything in an orderly progression from start to finish (whereas, for the line cooks responsible for the regular dining room, the orders come in seemingly at random and everything is bedlam). For a private party, you have to start the meat two courses before it's going to be served. But you must be prepared to delay things if the party is going slowly on account of people getting too festive or going outside for long cigarette breaks. And you need to be prepared to speed things up if, later on, they all of a sudden announce that they have to leave by a certain time. We had both experiences.

Twice, Matt had to "hold fire" (stop cooking) on the two whole beef tenderloins we had in the oven. Later, when the revelers revealed their secret deadline, Matt had to expropriate one of the pastry assistants to help us plate the cheese and dessert courses right away. It didn't seem to bother him. "Ha! This is nothing. The best is when six more people show up in the middle of the meal."

Downstairs, in the men's locker room, I peel off my now-dirty chef's whites (which will be laundered overnight in Long Island City and delivered to the restaurant at 6 A.M.). I engage a few of the cooks in a discussion of my foot problem. "Shit yeah, that's the hardest part of the job," they all seem to agree (the cooks spoke to me with some candor because Tom and Matt were the only ones who knew I was documenting the week—Tom thought having a writer around would make the cooks nervous, so they were told I was the chef's friend who's a lawyer and wants to spend a few days in the kitchen). One faction supports clogs as the best choice, while another favors clunky, black rubber-soled shoes of the cop-on-the-beat variety. Small, iconoclastic minorities speak out in favor of work boots and running shoes. One of the female cooks adds, from the hallway, "I've had good luck with support hose."

• • •

I considered support hose most seriously in the middle of the night one night while struggling against fatigue and lower back pain in order to keep up with Eric, Gramercy Tavern's main fish supplier. Eric is to the Fulton Fish Market what Modesto is to the Greenmarket. Eric's company, EMS (Early Morning Seafood), supplies fish to a select group of New York's top restaurants, including Gramercy Tavern and Union Pacific. (Try the halibut at both restaurants and you'll see how different the same fish can taste when prepared according to drastically different recipes.)

Matt and I (along with two of the cooks) meet Eric outside the Fulton Fish Market at 2 A.M. We enter a bizarre nighttime world where, under blazing arc-lamps, miniature forklifts zoom around like evil bumper cars with fangs, and large men with rusty hooks slung over their shoulders smoke cigarettes and drink coffee while tossing around 150-pound crates of fish like they're bags of feathers. I'm wearing work boots.

It's the first day of diver scallop season. Eric has just returned from Maine. He and his wife, Pat, drove up there the previous morning, spent all day on a boat with a team of divers who hand-harvest very large (eight to a pound, when shucked) scallops, and drove back all night with two big coolers of scallops in the trunk of their Volvo. At lunchtime, Gramercy Tavern will be serving New York's first diver scallops of the year.

We enter a small shed off to one side of the Market. Inside, six men in yellow slickers are butchering gray sole at an alarming rate. Three swift cuts and the fillet is off the fish. One more cut and the flesh separates from the skin. Matt and I look on in wide-eyed amazement. "Now those are some knife skills," he admits. When we next see Chef Tom and tell him that we spent the night at the Fulton Fish Market, he immediately asks, "Did you check out the guys with the knives?"

As we chase Eric around the Market, I can't help but conclude that people who purchase food for a living are faster than normal humans. Eric is frantically trying to find skate that meets his exacting standards. We visit a dozen vendors, and Eric keeps asking, "Is this the best skate you got?" Finally, one of Eric's friends says that a shipment is just coming out of JFK Airport and that the truck will arrive in forty minutes.

We sit on a couple of crates of frozen salmon (not destined for Gramercy Tavern, which uses only fresh fish) and eat some sandwiches (salami, cheddar cheese, olives, capers, and mustard on Balthazar's cranberry nut bread) that Matt and I prepared earlier. Eric looks at his sandwich. "What's with the fancy-schmantzy bread? Doesn't anybody use white bread anymore?" He takes a bite. "Hey, you know, this is pretty good."

I ask Eric what he does during the day. "Oh, Pat and I have a restaurant in Jersey." He senses my incredulity. "We don't sleep much." We finish our meal with some leftover Gramercy Tavern desserts.

At about 6:30 A.M., all the vendors in the Fulton Fish Market will pack up their trucks and depart. The sidewalk will be hosed down and almost all traces of the market will disappear. The space will be used as a parking lot for the South Street Seaport. You could walk through the lot by day and, eerily, never be aware of the market's existence. And one day it will all be gone: the city plans to relocate the Fulton Fish Market to a new facility in the Bronx.

Work boots are a total failure. I'm sticking with a combination of running shoes and Advil.

It's Tom Colicchio's night off and Matt is in command, so of course all the VIPs decide to show up at once. Within moments of opening the restaurant, an order ticket shoots out of the printer with a special notation at the bottom: "4 VIPs—Chefs from Restaurant Taillevent, Paris." Thirty seconds later, "3 VIPs—Kevin Costner and Friends," followed by, "7 VIPs—Friends of Chef Tom." Matt shrugs. "Same thing happened last week—David Bouley showed up, along with a bunch of other industry people. It's a conspiracy."

For me, this is the most interesting moment of the week. As a restaurant critic, I always wonder how much a restaurant can do to improve the cuisine for a VIP table. In the case of Gramercy Tavern, at least, the answer is: not much. VIP treatment at Gramercy Tavern basically consists of a little extra food. Perhaps the kitchen will send out half-portions of urchin between the appetizer and entree, or perhaps an extra dessert course. The actual preparation of the food, however, is unchanged. To Jonathan, on the line, it's just another order of foie gras. Or perhaps he spends an extra second selecting the specific piece of foie gras for the chefs from Taillevent. Looking at the foie gras orders coming over the pass, though, they all look the same to me. In one case, Matt walks over and prepares a dish himself, leaving Marco, another sous-chef (and now the head chef at Hearth, a restaurant in which Colicchio is an investor), in charge of the orders—but it seems mostly a symbolic gesture. The line cooks make these dishes all day. Matt's final product, for all his skill, can't possibly represent a substantial improvement.

Indeed, in the course of a week—during which I observe almost every order that goes through the kitchen—I never see any secret, special, VIP-only dishes or anything of that sort. The kitchen always keeps a piece of salmon on hand for one very special customer—but that's about it. Nor is every request from a VIP table granted.

A waiter reports, "245 wants four side-orders of escarole." Matt shakes his head. "What do I look like, I'm made of escarole here? Offer them spinach." He explains to me, "If I had it, I'd give it to them, but we make maybe one head of escarole for the whole dinner service." Technically, Gramercy Tavern doesn't even offer side dishes—but the kitchen tries hard to accommodate all customer requests, VIP or not. All night, shouts of "SOS" (sauce on the side), "All Meat" (no vegetables), and "Veg. Entree" (a vegetable plate) can be heard in the kitchen.

In five years at Gramercy Tavern, Matt has heard just about every special request in the book. "233, table of two, wants to do the tasting menu but wants a substitution for every course." I think Matt's head is going to explode, but he just says, "Fine. They can have whatever they want as long as they both get the same courses."

It's my last night in the kitchen. By now, my brunoise is almost good enough to satisfy Matt. "You're leaving? But we just got you trained," says one cook. "You're okay—for a lawyer," quips another. I'm just happy to be getting off my feet.

Back in the dining room, my wife, Ellen, and I are customers again, and my feet feel great. I'm sitting there, looking at my appetizer, wondering whether Jonathan made it . . . and whether he knew he was making it for me . . . and whether, if he knew, he would care. Does my order ticket say "2 VIPs—Former Gramercy Tavern kitchen flunky/food critic Steven Shaw and wife, Ellen," or am I just a regular civilian again? Who's on the pass? Is it a good night in the kitchen?

Ellen asks me what I think of my appetizer.

I take a close look.

"Nice brunoise."

Gramercy Tavern is emblematic of modern fine-dining restaurants in America, and represents a happy meeting of quality and quantity. Hundreds of people a night can eat at Gramercy Tavern, yet each customer is the beneficiary of excellent cooking. The Gramercy Tavern kitchen is a precision assembly line, and the restaurant is recognizable as a well-run corporation similar to those in most any field. But there are many other kinds of restaurants, from much larger operations that engage in relentless mass production and banquet-style service, to smaller chef-driven establishments where the chef has direct involvement in most every dish.

At Sandor's restaurant in Seagrove Beach, Florida, it's 5 P.M. and the electricity has just gone out. Most normal restaurants would simply close for the evening, but Sandor's is no normal restaurant.

Sandor Zombori was raised in a Hungarian orphanage in the 1950s. His dissident parents had been jailed, so he was considered the lowest of the low in a bad place at a bad time. But blessed with an Olympian's physique, the reflexes of a praying mantis, and an abundance of street smarts, he enjoyed wild success as an athlete, eventually becoming the judo champion of Europe, a member of the 1964 Hungarian Olympic team, and one of the only Europeans ever to defeat Japan's best martial artists. In 1969 he escaped Hungary, climbing over electrified fences and evading border patrols with shoot-to-kill orders, through Romania, Bulgaria, Yugoslavia, and Austria, where he was granted political asylum.

Sandor arrived in the United States with nothing, and was taken in off the streets by the now legendary restaurateur George Lang, also a Hungarian Jew, and given a job as a dishwasher. Soon after, he enlisted in the United States Army and did six tours of duty in Vietnam as a Green Beret, a Ranger, and a Special Forces diver. He sustained multiple gunshot wounds and acquired citizenship as a result of his military service. After assimilating just about every skill the armed forces had to teach, he went on to become a computer technician for private defense contractors, where he saved his money and bided his time until he could pursue his real dream—a dream inspired in part by his childhood of privation and in part by his mentor and idol Mr. Lang: becoming a chef.

He traveled to France and trained at Le Cordon Bleu, and then pursued formal pastry training at Ecole Lenotre. He started his culinary career as the lowliest kitchen helper at Jamin, working under the great Joel Robuchon. He then proceeded to apprentice in charcuterie, patisserie, and various other trades at small shops across France and particularly Alsace, where he wound up in the kitchen of the Michelin three-star Auberge de l'Ill.

Upon his return to the United States, still a few dollars away from being able to open a restaurant, he purchased an Italian pasta machine and set up a small artisanal pasta and sauce production company in Pensacola, Florida, called Pannonia Pasta. In the late 1980s, there was no other source of high-quality fresh pasta in that region of the Southeast, and Pannonia became the major pasta supplier in the area.

He opened the first Sandor's restaurant in 1991 in Pensacola, and was unhappy almost from opening day. The restaurant was too big, preventing Sandor (pronounced "SHON-door") from preparing the true European cuisine he wanted to provide to his guests. It was in a high-crime area, and there were at least four robbery incidents at Sandor's, including a hostage situation. (Sandor will not tell you this, but if you talk to various chefs in Pensacola they'll recount dramatic tales of how former Green Beret/martial arts champion Sandor, then in his fifties, disarmed a gang of hoodlums, rescued his waitress who was being held at knifepoint, and brought the surely bewildered bad guys to justice.)

He closed the original Sandor's in 1994 and relocated to Seagrove Beach a couple of hours east along the northwest Florida coast. This is the most remote area of Florida, the part few people outside the immediate region are familiar with—so far west it's in the Central time zone. There he built a thirty-two-seat restaurant (though he accepts only twenty-five reservations per night), which he operates to this day.

Sandor, in his neverending quest for self-improvement, closes his restaurant every January and visits kitchens around the world, especially in New York. He has done short stages at, among others, New York's Mix, Vong, Jean Georges, Le Bernardin, Cello, Lespinasse, and Tabla, collecting ideas and honing his technique. He is particularly close friends with Eric Ripert of Le Bernardin. "Growing up in Hungary, I never saw a fish. So I learned from Eric."

I met Sandor in the kitchen of Lespinasse in New York, where I was doing a week-long kitchen stage a few years ago. Sandor was doing the same, and we bonded over a baby pig. Ever since our week together, Sandor e-mailed me persistently and persuasively, asking that I visit Seagrove Beach and tell the world about the emerging restaurant culture in the area (little does Sandor know I have no such power).

A meal at Sandor's leaves you wondering what would happen if any of the top chefs from New York or Paris had to operate under similar conditions: there is only one person in Sandor's kitchen, and that is Sandor. There are no prep cooks, no line cooks, no sous-chefs. Most everything, from taking reservations and creating the wine list, to the preparation and cooking of all the hot dishes—most of which are based on the numerous stocks he prepares every day—is done by him. (Salads and a few other cold dishes are assembled by the servers.) There's a waiter and a waitress, though you can be sure that if Sandor could do it, he'd prefer to wait on every table as well. Sandor's wife, Mary, occasionally answers the phone. And one of the waitress's daughters comes in late some nights to help with the dishes.

One surreal March evening in Sandor's kitchen, I note at 5:45 P.M. that the temperature on the wall thermometer reads 85 degrees Fahrenheit. There is no air conditioning in this northwest Florida kitchen. Sandor, who has spent all day engaged in mise en place (the French kitchen term meaning "everything in its place" is utilized in most every restaurant to refer to prep work), has his entire arsenal of ingredients and tools at the ready, like a surgeon preparing to operate. He increases the burner and oven temperatures and waits for the first orders.

I've been playing out in my mind how Sandor will receive an order for a dish, obtain his ingredients, heat the main protein and track the various sauces and garnishes, and plate everything in a coordinated manner, when the waitress comes into the kitchen with an order not for one plate of food but for a four-course meal for a table of six. Within moments, Sandor, seemingly with six arms, fills the available counter space with empty plates, skillets, and pots—this meal will require the preparation of twenty-four dishes in all. Refrigerator and cabinet doors open and ingredients get placed in their cooking vessels. Sandor surveys the scene, performing a quick mental calculation of what needs to start cooking first so that all dishes will come out in the proper sequence. By 6 P.M. the thermometer is up to 92 degrees.

As the appetizers go out to the first table, orders come in for two additional tables. Sandor performs the same preparatory drill, all the while monitoring the progress of the second and third courses that are working on the stoves and in the ovens. He doesn't even break a sweat as the mercury climbs to 96 degrees at 6:30 P.M.

As the kitchen breaks 100 degrees soon after, Sandor is in the thick of service. At a peak moment, he might have as many as fifty different dishes in various stages of the preparation and cooking process. As a table's dishes are ready, always it seems at just the right time, Sandor builds each final plate rapidly, sending them out in pairs with his servers as he keeps building the rest. He can serve a table of six in less than a minute from the time he puts the first ingredient on the first plate to the time he touches up the garnish on plate number six.

By 8 P.M. the kitchen is 109 degrees. By 9 P.M., 116 degrees. "How high does it go, Sandor?" I ask, starting to feel unsteady.

"I don't know," he deadpans. "The thermometer only goes up to 120."

Sandor's restaurant, formerly an architect's office, is not a fancy building, but everything in the dining room is of high quality, from the chairs and the table linens to the flatware and the oil paintings of Napoleon that ring the room. Sandor, though he appears to be seven feet tall, is a major Napoleon buff, and has in his estimation read every book on Napoleon written in the five languages he speaks. "For me, Napoleon is about anything being possible, no matter who you are or where you come from."

On the night the power goes out, I have a reservation at Sandor's, as do twenty-five other people. As soon as power is lost, Sandor doesn't hesitate for an instant: the Green Beret instincts kick in and he develops a plan of action. Light will be provided by candles, flashlights, and hanging lanterns. Cooking is no problem: the stoves are gas-powered. As for refrigeration, while Sandor is cooking dinner, his wife, Mary, and several friends make multiple car trips to Sandor's home in order to place the products in his home refrigerators. Later, he is able to run a series of 100-foot-long extension cords to neighboring establishments to power some of his essential equipment.

Did I mention that, the previous day, Sandor had fired one of his two waiters?

At the end of the meal—which is as good as a meal at Sandor's under the best of circumstances—Sandor comes out into the dining room and pulls up a chair near our table. "Rough night?" I ask.

Sandor casts a disbelieving look my way. "Because of a little electrical problem?" he says. "That's hardly a rough night."

Sandor's seems tiny and Gramercy Tavern seems large by comparison, but there are restaurants that dwarf even Gramercy Tavern—places where customers per day are counted not in tens or hundreds but in thousands. How do they maintain quality on such a large scale? On Saturday, Valentine's Day 2004, my wife, Ellen, and I spend the morning at New York's famous Tavern on the Green restaurant observing the kitchen's brunch shift. There are 600 brunch reservations at Tavern today, and 2,500 dinner reservations. It's a big restaurant.

We begin early, in one of the prep areas, where we are placed under the guidance of Fernando, the sous-chef in charge of, among other things, eggs. Fernando is, in restaurant parlance, the "egg man." But, of course, he is not just any egg man. He is the egg man at one of the world's largest and best known restaurants, and he has been with Tavern for twenty-one years. No slouch is he when it comes to eggs.

Tavern uses Grade AA Extra Large eggs and they come by the case. Each case contains 30 dozen—360 eggs. Fernando estimates that today the restaurant will use seven cases for the brunch service. "On the busiest day," he says, "I might open fifteen cases. Or more."

The basic theory of poaching eggs, according to Fernando, is: "The yolks, they try to rise. The whites, they try to sink. When the egg goes in, if the white wraps around the yolk the yolk brings it back to the top and it's a good egg, round with a tail. If the white doesn't wrap around the yolk, either the yolk pops away or you make a fried egg on the bottom." Fernando repeatedly illustrates with his hands—occasionally employing his Krispy Kreme baseball hat as a prop—how the yolk and white need to come together just so.

The water bath in which the eggs are poached is about the size of the tubs they use at pet salons to bathe large-breed dogs. It is filled with water and vinegar and brought to a simmer. Fernando works with sixty eggs at a time. He places two trays (thirty eggs each) next to the water bath. The selection process begins at this point, as he discards any obviously damaged eggs. He then proceeds to crack the rest into the water bath with staggering speed, one hand feeding the eggs to the other hand as he cracks the eggs one-handed directly into the water bath. I clock him at twenty-six seconds for a tray. "If I go slow," Fernando says, "half the eggs cook before the other half are in." But at plus or minus thirteen seconds there is no worry of great variance. Fernando informally separates tray 1 from tray 2 by working at both ends of the water bath.

In order to avoid damage to the eggs as they enter the water, he cracks them very close to the water's surface. He then pulls away swiftly, a motion that helps the egg form its shape: a sphere with a tail of whites. At this point he begins culling the worst of the eggs, throwing them into the large garbage pail he keeps next to the poaching station for this purpose. There are a lot of eggs that break up or otherwise don't meet the standard, but most of them come out right.

The eggs will poach for around 3.5 minutes, Fernando says, and I hit my stopwatch. Fernando, amazingly, wanders off to do something else (he is also preparing lamb shanks for the dinner service). Fernando manages to get an entire tub full of lamb shanks into another gigantic bath-like contraption in less than the time it takes the eggs to poach.

He has never used a timer for poaching eggs, but it is almost exactly at the three-minute mark that he wanders back over to the poaching station and tests an egg. He also makes me press on the egg to see the right texture of a correctly poached egg.

It is now almost exactly 3.5 minutes into the poaching process, and he rapidly removes all the eggs with a wire mesh scoop and plunges them into tub of ice water. There are still a lot of imperfect eggs, even though at every stage of the process Fernando has discarded several flawed ones.

Fernando repeats this sixty-egg poach several times, and also continues to multitask with the lamb shanks. It only takes him about a half hour to poach several hundred eggs and finish browning the lamb shanks (later they will be braised in veal stock and red wine, this liquid will form the basis of the sauce, and they will be plated with creamy polenta).

One of Fernando's cooks then goes through the poached eggs that are sitting in the ice water and selects only the ones that are up to standard. Each of them has a tail of whites hanging off the spherical part of the egg. The assistant plucks these tails off by hand and lays the eggs in stainless trays, which are then covered and stacked.

Poaching is not the only use of eggs at Tavern on the Green, needless to say. There are scrambled eggs, par-cooked in a gigantic cauldron. There are crab cakes, which contain—in addition to jumbo lump crab meat, shredded crab meat, scallions, and seasonings—eggs in two forms: whole beaten eggs and a little mayonnaise. For Valentine's dinner, they are making heart-shaped mini crab cakes (for brunch, they are making larger round ones). There is French toast, par-cooked and heated to order at service. There is a frittata on the menu, and the eggs for that are cracked in advance. And, of course, when poached eggs are served they are most commonly made into eggs Benedict ("eggs Benny" in kitchen-speak), and that requires Hollandaise. In this case, about three hundred eggs worth of it.

Over in an adjacent room, they're washing spinach. The bags of spinach are dumped into the largest commercial sink I've ever seen. They are then moved around with a shovel, and removed with a big strainer into one of the greatest kitchen tools in the world: the cauldron-sized Salad Ace electric salad spinner–dryer. I also notice a garbage pail full of peeled potatoes. Maybe there will be french fries.

Fernando and his crew will now turn their attention fully to dinner prep. It's time for us to transfer the breakfast materials to the main kitchen, and for brunch service to begin.

Frank is in charge of the station that handles poached eggs, crab cakes, frittatas, and several other items. His first words to my wife are, "Don't I know you from somewhere?" And it turns out he does: ten years ago, Frank was the counterman at Canard & Co., the deli-grocery around the corner from our apartment. She used to buy coffee from him every day. He has been at Tavern for the past six years.

The orders come in on a little computer printer and the crew (Frank has two other cooks in his station, and there's also a roving sous-chef who checks in from time to time) starts to produce.

Frank has done some eggs Benny prep of his own: while Fernando was actually poaching the eggs, Frank was toasting English muffins and laying out slices of ham. Another cook—a man from Bangladesh who has been at Tavern since 1984—made the Hollandaise. Everything is laid out at Frank's station and shortly before the first orders come in, hot water is added to a tray of poached eggs to warm them.

Frank quickly assembles the orders as they come in. He puts each plate under a broiler briefly to heat the muffin and give the ham (which is already cooked) a little color. He then adds the eggs, sauce, and garnish, and places the eggs on the "pass" where they are given a final sprinkling of herbs. A lid is then placed on the plate to keep it warm as a runner carries it down the long hallways and through the sprawling premises to its final destination.

The end result is a great plate of eggs Benny, with the poached eggs nicely liquid at the center.

Farther along the line, another cook is preparing the day's special frittata. These are cooked to order, and are a bit like omelettes but are not folded. The frittata du jour is crabmeat, potato, and asparagus, topped with cheddar. The cook begins with the fillings in a small skillet, adds an egg mixture, and uses a combination of shaking, tossing, and a rubber spatula to get the eggs into an almost-done state, at which point he sprinkles cheddar on top and places it under a broiler to finish and fluff a bit.

The French toast and scrambled egg stations are also cranking.

I was wondering what had happened to all that spinach, and it turns out that on another station it is being used as a garnish for two of the more lunch-like brunch dishes, salmon and chicken.

And I finally get my french fries, which, by the way, are outstanding: cut fresh and fried twice.

On the way out, I check in with Fernando's crew in the prep kitchen. They're boiling up some special Valentine's Day ravioli. Fernando is happy—he's going on vacation tomorrow.

Compared to the cacophonous bazaar of a restaurant's main kitchen line, the pastry kitchen in most any fine restaurant is like a Tibetan monastery. Pastry chefs are, on the whole, the academics of the culinary world, their methods requiring great precision, their recipes like scientific formulas, and their emphasis almost entirely on the transformation of ingredients.

One of the more embarrassing events of my life is the day I spend with Chris Broberg, now the pastry chef at Café Gray, in his subterranean pastry kitchen at Lespinasse. No monk-scientist am I, so I start the morning by over-mixing a batch of batter that could have made about 1,500 delicious cookies. Pastry chefs have their own vocabulary, and despite repeated explanations and even photographic references in a pastry text, I can't figure out when the batter has reached the right consistency. It's 5 A.M. and already I'm in the hole.

My big project for the morning is to make the fruit

tarts, supposedly the simplest job available in the pastry kitchen. It's the job they give to culinary-school interns and new, untrained employees. Broberg's fruit tarts are one of his signatures, and bear little resemblance to the flat, round, flaky-crusted fruit tarts typically sold at pastry shops. Rather, his tarts are about three inches tall, made with a crumb crust, stuffed with fruit, and capped with more crust, and shaped like an eye.

I'm sent back to the dreaded Hobart mixer, similar to the KitchenAid mixers used by many home cooks but with twenty times the capacity, this time with the instruction to mix the crust dough until it's "like little pellets." Broberg has learned his lesson: he watches over my shoulder and gently points out when I should stop the mixer.

The eye-shaped molds, which Broberg had made for him by a metalcrafter, then need to be lined with the crumb dough. "It's easy," declares Broberg. "Just make sure it's the same thickness all around and that there aren't any gaps, otherwise it will crack. And don't press too hard or the crust will be too hard and chewy." He demonstrates, and in about thirty seconds he has used his fingers to press a uniform layer of crumb crust against the sides of the mold and across the bottom where the mold meets the sheet pan. Ten minutes later, I finish my first one. Only thirty-six more to go.

It takes me most of the morning to get twenty-five of them done, at which point Broberg swoops in and finishes the rest in a few minutes. He then makes a dozen extras, just in case some of mine aren't up to standard. After the tarts have been filled with the day's fruit selection, pears and pear liqueur, we bake and, later, unmold them. It's not hard to tell which trays of tarts are Broberg's and which are mine, but enough of mine come out well that the evening's dessert service will be covered.

Later I ruin an entire sheet-pan full of mini-eclairs. I can't seem to get the chocolate coating to adhere, even though I follow Broberg's motions as exactly as I can. He can't figure out what I'm doing wrong either. "It usually works," he shrugs.

By the end of the day, I even manage to mismeasure ingredients on a scale designed to be idiotproof.

All these things would cause the typical chef to become irate. Pastry chefs tend to be made of different stuff, though. No matter how many stupid mistakes I make, Chris is simply amused and matter-of-factly corrects my mistakes as he goes about his business. It probably helps that the basic ingredients of pastry—flour, sugar, butter, and eggs—are cheap. Though they are labor intensive, in terms of food cost pastry offerings are the highest profit-margin items on most restaurant menus. Although the best chocolate, real vanilla beans, and a few other pastry ingredients carry high price tags, overall a fine dining restaurant might have a savory food cost of 30 percent (in other words an appetizer plus entree totaling $50 would cost the restaurant $15 in ingredients) and a dessert food cost of closer to 10 percent.

When it comes time to serve the fruit tarts at dinner, Chris will have been home for several hours already. Two pastry assistants will handle the heating of the intentionally undercooked tarts and will then devote themselves to building the tart into a complete restaurant dessert. The eye-shaped pear tart will be placed in a precise circle of pear sauce in the middle of a plate. Slices of poached pear and a vanilla crème anglaise will encircle the tart. And atop the tart will be two quenelles of ice cream and sorbet, vanilla and pear respectively.

At the top restaurants, where pastry chefs like Broberg represent the pinnacle of the industry, American pastry artistry is at an all-time high. Even more so than in the savory part of the kitchen, it is not uncommon for top European pastry chefs to come to America to learn from our best. Lately, in the larger cities there have even arisen niche dessert-only restaurants like Finale in Boston, Sugar Dessert Bar in Chicago, and ChikaLicious in New York City. Yet despite these successes, there's a feeling in the pastry chef community that pastry chefs are something of an endangered species.

Frequent diners are, after all, often like me: they're never actually hungry and they have enough body fat reserves to last a month or so on a life raft. Pastry chefs are up against a huge challenge when trying to tempt such customers, especially since they don't get their turn until after the savory part of the kitchen has already overfed the customer. A pastry chef can work to provide a dessert that fits naturally into the meal. But how many savory chefs try to create a meal that leads naturally to dessert-as-conclusion? It can be done—a meal can (and should) be engineered such that a sweet item becomes inevitable at the end. But this is rarely understood or even acknowledged by chefs, who mostly think of their pastry departments as subcontractors brought in to do an unpleasant job. I've found this to be the case less in France, where the executive chefs tend to be more involved in the desserts.

· · ·

Thus far, I've spoken of what would be considered fine-dining restaurants. But the same kind of care that Sandor, Chris Broberg, the Gramercy Tavern team, and the Tavern on the Green team exercise in preparing haute cuisine is exhibited every day in the best of the small, local, casual restaurants serving everything from hot dogs to pizza. It's this ethic of striving for excellence that separates the great pizzerias from Domino's and the great hot dog stands from the 7-11. In Connecticut, three such restaurants are examples that stand in stark contrast to the uncaring uniformity of so many chains and the restaurants that imitate them. They're the kinds of restaurants I look for when I choose where to dine out in any town: the idiosyncratic ones that may not be on the strip, may not have a fifty-foot-high sign, aren't part of a chain or trying to be like one, and are run with the same dedication and individualism as the best of the fine dining restaurants.

On Wooster Street in New Haven, Connecticut, two pizzerias have for decades been locked in sometimes amiable, sometimes not so amiable competition. Many people assume the best pizza in America is in New York City, or perhaps Chicago, but there is a sizable group of aficionados who think it's in New Haven, at Sally's Apizza (pronounced "uh-beets," reflecting the dialect of Catania, Sicily) and Frank Pepe Pizzeria Napoletana, known locally just as Sally's and Pepe's. My credentials as a patriotic New Yorker are second-to-none, but I agree with those aficionados.

What makes these places so special are the same things that make any restaurant tower over its peers: people who care, a tradition of excellence, the best ingredients, and a well-run operation. Sally's and Pepe's have been pulling this off since before World War II. When a restaurant you've never heard of has a line out the door despite looking like a military fortification, there's probably something going on. In the South it might be a great barbecue or fried chicken restaurant; in Texas it might be a taco place; but in New Haven, Connecticut, it's all about pizza.

Frank Pepe's bakery opened its doors in 1925, though at that time it sold not exactly pizza but rather pizza-like tomato pies (some reports indicate that he was selling these tomato pies from a horse-drawn cart much earlier). It moved to larger digs across the parking lot in 1934. Frank Pepe's nephew, Sal Consiglio, opened Sally's up the block in 1938.

Sally's pizza oven is surely one of the wonders of the pizza world: ancient, brutally dry and hot, spewing forth sparks, flames, and smoke with reckless abandon. The bakers, or stick men, who are the sons of current owner Flo Consiglio (widow of the departed founder, Sal Consiglio), use seven-foot-long peels to slide the pizza onto the tiny hearth (for nobody who wishes to live gets very close to this evil monster) and to manipulate the baking pies around the oven's hot and cold spots so as to avoid uneven cooking. Sally's bakers, at the end of the day, look as though they've been working the boiler room of the Titanic.

Sally's pies are cooked at relatively high temperatures, in excess of 700 degrees Fahrenheit, and they emerge from the oven scalding hot, irregularly shaped squarish ovals served on wax paper–lined rectangular metal trays, with a just-charred cornmeal-studded and blistered crust, fragrant tomato sauce, and bubbling mozzarella cheese. Sally's is often so crowded that people wait on line an hour or more to get in, and another hour for their pizza.

Up the block at Pepe's, as at Sally's, coals get added to the oven prior to and throughout service. The oven never goes out, but burns cooler overnight and on Tuesdays when the restaurant closes. When service begins, as Gary Bimonte, the grandson of Frank Pepe, explained it to me, they have a four-step production process for making pizza. On the right-hand side of the kitchen stands the "pizza man." This is the person who forms the dough into the round pizza shape. On the left is the "decorator," who adds whatever sauce, cheese, and toppings need to be added. When the pies are ready to go into the oven they fall under the authority of the "oven man," in this case Gary Bimonte. Once they are removed from the oven the "coordinator" directs them to tables or into takeout boxes.

When the stations are double- and triple-staffed, the restaurant is able to create as much as a pie per minute at peak times. On a visit to New Haven, Gramercy Tavern sous-chef Matt Seeber remarks, "We need some of these guys in our kitchen."

Nearby, in Fairfield, Connecticut, Gary Zemola mans the grill at his hot dog stand, The Super Duper Weenie. Zemola, like many of the chefs at the top fine-dining restaurants, is a Culinary Institute of America graduate and formerly the chef at Pasta Nostra, a well-regarded Italian restaurant in South Norwalk, Connecticut. Zemola began by selling frankfurters out of a 1973 GMC Stepvan in the parking lot of the Fairfield Lighting Center, right off I-95. The Super Duper Weenie logo—a superhero character with blond hair and a red-and-blue uniform—came with the truck, which was originally owned by Robert Sterner and was purchased from subsequent owners and lovingly restored by Zemola in 1992. He now has a small shop—just eight seats at the counter and a few picnic tables outside—in the very same spot, and is in the process of opening two additional shops along I-95.

His approach to hot dogs is the same as any chef's approach to any dish. He ascertains what makes a frankfurter good, what is the best way to cook it, and what are the best condiments. He works with an outside vendor who accepts a custom order and manufactures the frankfurters to his specifications regarding meat, seasoning, and casing. He cooks each in a consistent and professional manner, on a carefully regulated and regularly cleaned grill, each frankfurter slit down the middle to increase the amount of crispy surface and facilitate the insertion of a piece of bacon if requested. And he precisely engineers and hand-makes all condiments, applying them in thoughtful combinations to enhance the dogs by creating counterpoints of flavor, temperature, and texture. He orders great rolls, too, from a nearby Portuguese bakery. In short, he cares.

On our drive home from our New Haven pizza expedition, Matt Seeber and I grab a hot dog at Super Duper Weenie. "We should hire this guy, too," he muses.

In all cases, the scale and resources of fine-dining kitchens have an impact on their abilities. Sandor is able to prepare every dish himself, but he must make compromises in terms of the small number of people he can serve and the level of complexity he can offer on any given plate. Gramercy Tavern combines the assembly line with traditional craftsmanship so as to produce a happy middle ground where the goals of culinary artistry can inhabit the same space as a business's desire to feed a lot of customers. Tavern on the Green, at its scale, must tend toward the less romantic vision of the industrial mass-production facility: there is a certain level of quality beyond which such a kitchen cannot advance, yet it can provide thousands of people with very good food.

Knowing what goes on behind the scenes in restaurants at all levels is, I think, a key to making good dining choices and establishing reasonable expectations. Chefs, kitchens, restaurateurs, and restaurants come in every size and at every level of ambition. Every combination has its limitations, and sometimes it's a wonder that they work at all.

There is a certain pure joy to eating food from the small, focused kitchens of cooks like Gary Zemola of Super Duper Weenie. In his own way, he provides one of the most consistently excellent culinary experiences imaginable: he does a few things, and he does them as well as they can be done. A fine restaurant like Gramercy Tavern, where the kitchen is ultimately a type of factory, can never approach that level of minimalist perfectionism. Your neighborhood family-run Chinese restaurant, meanwhile, where mom and pop cook every dish themselves in an ancient wok, may have the edge, in consistency and experience, over a four-star restaurant.

At the same time, there is a limit to what the solo kitchen can accomplish, in both scale and complexity. What you're paying for in a fine-dining restaurant is a certain level of sophistication in cuisine that can be as intellectually stimulating as art, and an experience that goes beyond food to include service, ambiance, and a host of intangibles.

As a lover of all cuisine, I get a thrill from the best examples of the output of all kinds of restaurants and kitchens. Unfortunately, too many people don't. There are the snobs, those who think of anything but fine dining as inferior. There are the reverse-snobs, those who think fancy restaurants are only for dilettantes and, even worse, French people. But really, every restaurant is for everyone who is willing to love it for what it is. Assuming, that is, you can afford it.

CHAPTER THREE

Food Sources and Controversies

"When David Burke came up with the Bronx Chop, nobody in the industry knew what the hell he was talking about." Philip Mosner, representing the middle of three generations of Mosners in his family's veal-packing business, grabs one of several dozen veal legs suspended from the ceiling on stainless steel hooks, hefts it onto his shoulder, brandishes a foot-long, curved butchering knife, and gestures for us to follow him to the cutting table. In an attempt to avoid being struck by the arcing leg as Mosner turns, I back into the front half of a veal carcass. It feels like a firm pillow, or maybe I just wish it does: I got up before six in the morning to make this meeting. Mosner moves rapidly and I scurry to keep up for fear of getting lost in the 700,000 square feet of refrigerated meat lockers at the Hunts Point Cooperative Market in the South Bronx.

The invention of a new cut of veal—the "Bronx Chop," a signature dish at chef David Burke's New York restaurant davidburke & donatella—may not immediately strike the carnivore community as significant. But in the meat business, it's one of those seemingly unattainable achievements, like cold fusion, perpetual motion, or the fountain of youth. *Veal Dish*, the veal industry newsletter published by the National Cattlemen's Beef Association, devoted an issue almost in its entirety to Burke and Mosner's collaboration. In the short time I spend in Michael Mosner's office (Philip's brother, Michael, is president of the company), a call comes in: it's a chef (and *Veal Dish* subscriber) in Pennsylvania asking about the Bronx Chop.

As Chef Burke and I lean in to watch Philip Mosner carve the Bronx Chop out of the veal leg, a group of other butchers gathers around to observe. I'm a bit excited as well, so much so that I briefly forget how cold my feet are: it's 36 degrees in the Mosner Veal facility—a piece of data that hadn't been provided to me when I set up this appointment. The butchers are wearing insulated boots and down coats under their white aprons; I'm wearing a cotton sweater and Sperry Top Siders.

"Every time I see a veal leg," enthuses Burke as Mosner puts the leg through a series of contortions designed to remove a softball-size piece of meat from near the hip joint, "I notice this great piece of meat right at the top. And it's totally wasted: most places just cut it up into cutlets." Mosner pulls a hunk of flesh out of the leg and holds it up like the triumphant father in *The Lion King*, while I marvel at his ability to be so upbeat at seven in the morning. He then takes it over to a band saw and starts cutting away the extraneous bones and fat. Finally, the Bronx Chop emerges: it looks like a colossal filet mignon, but with a primeval bone attached, reaching for the sky. There's only one Bronx Chop per veal hindquarter—two per whole calf—and Burke serves 180 of them in his restaurant each week. "People are going to eat this at my restaurant," predicts Burke. "They're going to remember it, and they're going to come back for it."

Philip Mosner and David Burke aren't the only people toiling silently to bring you that Bronx Chop. The tender veal they butcher, distribute, cook, and serve is a result of careful breeding and agricultural research. The specific calves used by Mosner are raised on a farm in Quebec, where a group of small farmers in Charlevoix are pioneers in the humane raising of excellent quality veal. The calves have room to move about and interact with one another, they are fed no hormones or sub-therapeutic doses of antibiotics, and the care with which they're treated is evident on the palate—the meat isn't cheap, but it's worth it. The calves are processed (a nice way of saying slaughtered) at the Abattoir Bellerive, also in Quebec, at which point they receive a U.S. Department of Agriculture inspection stamp—USDA inspectors are on hand to certify meat that is destined for cross-border shipment. At this point, the logistics industry enters the picture, moving the veal carcasses overnight by truck to Mosner's receiving room.

Mosner's multistage operation begins with whole carcasses and, step by step, breaks them down into the various cuts of veal a restaurant or local butcher shop might buy: shanks, shoulders, top rounds, 5- to 8-bone racks, whole breasts, tenderloins, and, of course, the Bronx Chop. Mosner has its own fleet of delivery trucks, but it sells most of its meat to "jobbers," which are small delivery fleets that service local restaurants and butchers. Once the meat reaches Burke's restaurant, his on-site butcher further trims the Bronx Chop into two portions: the large, dramatic piece that will sell for $36 on the dinner menu, and a smaller boneless cut that will be served at lunchtime. By the time a waiter carries the Bronx Chop to the customer's table, it has passed through two different cooking stations and in the process has picked up some pistachio ravioli, wild mushrooms, and a sauce.

As I spend most every waking moment dwelling on culinary matters (that is, when I'm not worrying about how to pay the next phone bill), I've been drawn repeatedly to topics of food sources because they are so obviously fundamental to cuisine. What separates an average restaurant from a good one is, in part, ingredients. What I look for in a restaurant is high quality. Unfortunately, most restaurants today use food of indiscriminate quality provided by high-volume vendors like Sysco and U.S. Foodservice, where the emphasis is on low price.

This chapter is a celebration of food that isn't coming from the giant meat plants in Colorado or off of the big trucks. It's about artisanal and small, high-quality farmers and producers of everything from cheese to clams to herbs, and chefs and purveyors who deal in quality. Beginning close to my home and reaching as far as British Columbia, I've explored many of the sources of the food we eat in restaurants. My hope is that for those who care enough to ask, and to explore, enjoyment of restaurant meals can be enhanced manyfold by the knowledge of all that happens before the plate hits the table. If you're conversant with the sources of food, from agriculture and aquaculture to production and processing, you can not only heighten your appreciation but also look at menus and restaurants with a more critical eye.

The examination of food sources also entails a discussion of some of the many controversies surrounding modern agriculture and eating habits. In the course of talking to farmers, fishers, producers, and processors, I've learned not just about ingredients but also about the many perspectives on and stories behind these controversies. Throughout this chapter, I offer a skeptical examination of some of the scientific and moral claims we hear about food, from governments, organizations, media, and restaurants—claims that some foods and production methods are categorically good for us and the world, while others aren't.

A restaurant menu is a document not only about the finished dishes you will be served but also about sources. Over the past couple of decades, there has been a trend—a welcome trend for the most part—toward discussing ingredients in detail on menus. This trend reached an absurd peak in the mid-1990s, when it seemed that menu descriptions were becoming more like food essays than descriptions of dishes. But while it's easy to poke fun at the excesses of menu descriptions, fundamentally information is a good thing, so long as we can figure out which information is important.

In much of Europe, where the culinary and agricultural traditions have been long entrenched, there is a regulated vocabulary for describing dishes. When a menu says *Poularde de Bresse*, you know you are getting a chicken from the Bresse region of France. You also know that any chicken with that designation has been raised to exacting standards of feed, space to roam, and more, all administered by a governing body. And you know exactly what kind of chicken you're getting: the regulations are such that a *Poularde de Bresse* will have a weight of around 1.8 kilograms and will be 5 months old. But the smaller, younger *Poulet de Bresse* will weigh around 1.2 kilograms and will be 4 months old, whereas the *Chapon de Bresse* will weigh in near 3 kilograms and will be 8 months old. There are thousands of European ingredients governed by such regulations and nomenclature guidelines.

In the United States, there is no such regime of standardized language, so menu descriptions, to be meaningful, must usually be longer. Unfortunately, length and specificity do not always contribute to meaning. But an aware consumer can identify the pertinent menu language and dismiss the rest, or at least know what questions to ask. Reputable brand names, like Niman Ranch and Coleman Natural beef, are the closest we have to a surrogate for the European system, and when reading menus I pay close attention to such descriptions. If I've never heard of the brand, I'll ask about it or do some research.

There are many products, such as beef and tuna, that often receive confusing or even disingenuous treatment on menus. The designation "USDA beef," while often used on menus, is meaningless, because all meat sold commercially in the United States must be approved by the U.S. Department of Agriculture (even imported beef is subject to USDA inspection and approval). The term "ahi tuna" doesn't designate a type or quality of tuna; it is a Hawaiian designation for tuna—the use of which is not standardized. Instead, look for real information. USDA Prime beef is a meaningful designation because only the best beef can receive the Prime designation. Likewise, beef that is dry aged (as opposed to wet aged or not aged at all) makes for more deeply flavored and tender steaks. USDA Prime dry-aged beef is the pinnacle of steak. Just plain USDA beef could be anything. Yellowfin and bluefin tuna are actual types of tuna, with the bluefin usually being richer and more desirable (and expensive). Ahi tuna could be either, or even another kind of tuna such as the less desirable albacore. More generally, menus throw around terms like "natural" and "low carb" without reference to any real standards. They are even prone to label vegetable oils "cholesterol free" when there is no such thing as cholesterol in a vegetable anyway. When you see such language on a menu, ask about it. If in the answer you get you sense marketing hype and cynicism rather than a commitment to quality, express your disappointment.

While there is value in information, some menus and restaurant marketing campaigns have become agenda-driven or overtly political: they take positions against genetically modified foods or in favor of organic ones, presume to make medical judgments about what is "heart healthy," or advertise participation in conservation programs that involve boycotts and lobbying efforts. Almost invariably, such highly touted ingredients come with higher price tags, and they may not taste better, so it pays to be familiar with and to examine the assumptions underlying such menu claims. Still other restaurants, such as vegetarian, macrobiotic, or raw food ones, have a specific food-ethics claim as their menu's raison d'etre. You may in the end choose to embrace any or all of those claims, but it's best to do so as a matter of informed choice after examining the issues.

Restaurant menus and personal choices are one thing, but governments in many instances also regulate what foods we are allowed to eat and at what price, through health regulations, import regulations, or economic incentives that encourage the production of one food or another. To many consumers, this is no big deal, but to food lovers it can be a major issue, as when regulations forbid the production of the best cheeses.

Now, I'm a city boy. It was not until recently, when I was called upon to teach a class about egg cookery, that I even knew the answers to basic questions like "Does a hen need to have sex with a rooster in order to lay an egg?" (The answer, by the way, is no.) But it's not as though New York City is particularly remote from food sources and producers: the Hudson River Valley is one of the finest growing regions for all manner of produce and livestock.

Take cheesemaker Jonathan White and his Bobolink Dairy in Vernon, New Jersey—traffic permitting, only about a ninety-minute drive from my apartment on the Upper East Side of Manhattan. Jonathan's land is right on the border between New York and New Jersey. Jonathan is one of America's foremost cheesemakers, yet every day he struggles against questionable regulations in order to bring us the best cheeses he can. He knows he could make even better cheeses if the regulations allowed him to use unpasteurized milk in his soft, Brie-like products, the way they do in France.

We begin my visit in the milking barn at around 8 A.M., which required a 6:30 A.M. departure from Manhattan. (I've lost count of the lost hours of early morning sleep I suffered as a result of writing this book, but apparently 8:00 A.M. is on the late side for dairy farmers.) Jonathan introduces me to each cow—his "ladies," as he calls them—by name.

It's impossible to overemphasize how well Jonathan treats his animals. He rescued many of them from factory farms and nursed them back to health. You can see it in their bearing and attitude, and especially in the behavior of the happy and inquisitive calves. I've found, contrary to my urban preconceptions of farmers as brutal slayers of beasts, that common to all the best farms I've visited is an abiding love and respect for the animals.

The calves feed out of a simulated-udder contraption imported from New Zealand (much of the equipment for the kind of sustainable farming and grass-feeding that Jonathan practices comes from Down Under). I learn that feeding milk to calves is actually uncommon in the industrial dairy sector.

Inside the dairy, the curds are cut with a multibladed steel contraption that looks like an evil harp. When Jonathan decides it's time to put the curds in molds, most of the whey is drained off (it will be fed to the calves or, sometimes, made into ricotta). Today Jonathan is making blue cheese, so to the drained curds he adds salt and bits of bread containing wild cultures. An entire day's milking at Jonathan's farm currently makes eight blue cheese wheels of about ten pounds each. He will grow (the farm is still young and he is expanding the herd), but not by much. He is, to use the popular buzzword of gourmet food today, artisanal.

The newly made cheeses go on racks in the dairy for a day or two, and then they get moved into Jonathan's ripening room, which is one of the neatest places on the planet to hang out, filled with seven-foot-high racks of wheels, pyramids, and other oddly shaped cheeses.

Of the seven or eight cheeses we taste, three are better than any cheese I've had in the United States and as good as any I've had in Europe, and all are at least superlative. These are all raw-milk cheeses, aged the legally required sixty days (longer for blue, cheddar, and the like). Unfortunately, the one thing you will not find on Jonathan's farm are young unpasteurized-milk cheeses in the style of the best French cheeses, like Brie, Camembert, and Epoisses. This is a product of nothing more than legislation, and in my opinion foolish legislation at that.

My obsession with illegal cheese began a decade ago, in France. "Why is this Camembert so much better than the Camembert in America?" I naively asked the waiter at Maisons de Bricourt in Brittany. "Because, Monsieur, it is made from—how do you say?—*lait cru*?" Deliberations ensued among the waitstaff. They delivered the verdict: "Row milk!"

Images of dilapidated alcoholic cows drinking malt-liquor out of paper bags sprung to mind, but eventually we determined that what he meant was raw milk. Unpasteurized milk. Milk straight from the cow, still harboring all the wonderful bacteria that constitute the soul of great cheese. But it is this very rawness that makes the cheese illegal.

A Frenchman invented the process that ruined most of the world's cheese, but it took the ingenuity of the U.S. Food and Drug Administration to mandate pasteurization of just about everything.

It is legal to use unpasteurized milk in cheese only if that cheese is aged more than sixty days (most potentially harmful bacteria die in this time). Tragically, this rules out all the young Brie, Camembert, and Epoisses (most of which are aged around thirty days) that many consider to be the pinnacle of the cheese-making art. Steven Jenkins, author of the *Cheese Primer* and perhaps America's leading authority on cheese, calls the pasteurized Brie and Camembert available in America, "pretenders—inauthentic impostors bearing their names."

Still, there are fabulous raw-milk cheeses available—like Jonathan White's—that have been aged for over sixty days. But just because something is legal doesn't mean it's easy to produce. Artisan raw-milk cheese-makers to whom I've spoken say that FDA inspectors pay "extra special attention" to their facilities, and, according to a number of recent articles in the professional cheese press, a forthcoming round of proposed FDA regulations will seek to outlaw raw-milk cheeses altogether—even those aged more than sixty days.

The ostensible fear is listeria, a food-borne bacterium that the FDA says can, when the planets are in alignment, kill pregnant women, infants, the elderly, and the otherwise infirm. But how serious is this threat? Are mothers really feeding raw-milk Camembert to their babies? And why not rely on rigorous inspection and informed consumer choice? It's hard to believe that raw-milk cheeses are as dangerous as, say, cigarettes, motorcycles, or even crossing the street.

Nor is cheese the only potential source of listeria—it can come from many food products, and, moreover, pasteurization is not a guarantee against listeria because the cheese can contract the bacteria even after treatment. I have consumed at least a hundred pounds of raw-milk cheese in the past few years, both in Europe where it's legal and here when I've been lucky enough to acquire some contraband; it is my testimony that the listeria threat is overblown. And, as the French are fond of taunting—and they're right—historically the most severe outbreaks of listeria have occurred in countries where young raw-milk cheeses are illegal, like America.

Of course, the government is not entirely to blame. Accomplice liability for the murder of cheese certainly belongs to the laziness of the large industrial cheese producers (it is far easier for them to pasteurize than to ensure that they only use wholesome milk in the first place) and the unimaginative American palate (which in large part is satisfied with bland cheeses). We get the cheese we deserve, and as long as Cheez Whiz outsells chevre a powerful anti-pasteurization lobby is not likely to form. But there are small steps the restaurant customer and food consumer can take. When you select cheeses from a restaurant's cheese cart, find out which ones are made from raw milk. If you travel to Europe or even Quebec and have a chance to eat raw-milk Brie, Camembert, or Epoisses, ask yourself if it's better. If it is, you may want to voice your support for regulatory change.

Jonathan White is one kind of farmer, but there are also farms that exist not on land but in the sea. Today, much of the seafood we eat in restaurants is the product not of old-style fishing but of modern aquaculture.

In Charleston, South Carolina, while visiting with chef Frank McMahon at the famous Hank's seafood restaurant, I overhear a sous-chef on the phone placing an order with his clam farmer. Clam farmer?

Several cell-phone calls later, we're in touch with Tony Blanchard of Blanchard's Seafood (also known as Stella

Maris Premium Seafood, named for the local church in Tony's nearby home town—it means "star of the sea"). "You want to come out and see us rake clams?" Tony says, somewhat incredulously. "Who did you say you write for again?" (Throughout the agricultural sector, there is an underlying suspicion that any journalist is going to turn out to be a shill for animal rights, ecology, or other causes that affect farmers' livelihoods.)

We arrive on the dock and, while we go to look for Tony and his crew, I speculate about which boat we'll be going out on. Will it be the majestic *Miss Ella*? Or perhaps the *Warrior*. As it turns out, those are actually shrimp boats. Nothing so grand is required for harvesting clams: the boat we wind up using looks like a spare part tied up to one of the larger boats. We go out in a questionable looking 21-foot skiff with an outboard motor. But with this small boat, Tony and three employees are able to maintain 10 million clams under cultivation, in 10' x 50' beds containing approximately 25,000 clams each.

Today we are to go out to a "purging bed" to retrieve one bed worth of clams. The night before, at low tide, the crew went out and raked the clams from the muddy bed, placed them in nets, and took them out to a clean, sandy-bottomed area near shore so they would purge out all the mud and grime they had accumulated. Not all clam harvesting operations bother with this purging phase (nor do all chefs approve of purging) but Blanchard's is a premium purveyor and his customers expect clams that are free of grit. They get a few cents more per clam, because they take extra steps to make a better product. In addition to purging, they grow their clams partially submerged (in other words, they are exposed at low tide) rather than fully submerged, and the South Carolina waters are cooler than those in, for example, Florida. This causes slower growth and therefore thicker shells, which means the clams will survive shipping better (Blanchard's best clams are sold mostly to establishments in New York and Boston).

The crew hauls the nets from the water and transfers the clams into plastic baskets. I try to help, but lack the physical strength to manipulate a thousand waterlogged clams one-handed on an unsteady boat with a slippery deck. I do, however, admire several clams.

What I learn from Tony Blanchard is that by looking at a clam's shell you can tell much about it. For example, a zig-zag pattern on the shell (as opposed to a pattern of concentric curves) is an indication that this clam comes from a genetically modified strain. The zig-zags only occur in a miniscule percentage of natural clams, but the genetically modified ones have it programmed in as an identification mechanism. The zig-zag will only be visible for a short time—once the clam dries, it can't be seen. Also, changes in a clam's environment will affect the growth rings. Tony could tell from looking at one clam that it had first been at the hatchery, then planted in a bed, and then probably replanted in another because, when first harvested, it was too small to sell.

As we're heading back in on the boat, Tony is on the cell phone with his distributor, the Lowcountry Lobster company. They will have a truck waiting to take the clams away as soon as they are ready.

The clams, once ashore, are sorted. The clams we commonly hear about—little neck, top neck, cherrystone, etc.—are actually all the same species, called *Mercenaria mercenaria*. The specific names are size gradations.

The sorting machine is a great toy. The clams go into a hopper, after which the machine is activated. Several sets of rollers are stacked one atop another, each with a different size gap. The largest clams get kept on the top level of rollers, the next size down fall through and get trapped by the next set of rollers, and so on. The smallest ones—the "replants"—fall all the way through into a trough. They'll be taken back out to the beds and grown for another six months or so. The different sets of rollers feed into different tubes, which sort the clams into different buckets. Tony's guys use calipers periodically to confirm the accuracy of the sorter.

As promised, while the sorting and grading process is occurring, the driver from Lowcountry Lobster arrives. Local restaurants will get these clams same-day and a delivery will go up to New York by truck for arrival tomorrow or the next day. These clams will last for a couple of weeks under careful refrigeration, but they are best if consumed sooner. The guys bag up the clams for the Lowcountry Lobster driver, and off he goes.

That night, I enjoy a bowl of Blanchard's clams, cooked up by Frank McMahon in the style of a bouillabaisse. They are delicious: meaty, fresh, and free of grit. Unlike farmed salmon, clams farmed using these "mariculture" methods taste the same as wild clams—at least to me they do.

Blanchard's is the kind of operation I like to see. The four guys I spend the morning with—Tom Metherell, John Benton, Chaz Green, and Tony Blanchard—are highly educated about seafood. They participate in several sustainable local aquaculture programs, but they embrace modern technology where appropriate. Having seen the cleanliness and transportation efficiency of this operation, I have far more confidence eating raw clams in New York.

Though often thought of as being its own species, wine is also a kind of food: the grapes are grown by farmers and processed into a product that restaurants serve. It is, along with cheese and bread, one of our most ancient foods, handed down from the earliest civilizations and passed on to us from our Old World forbears.

In the New World, in Oregon, winemaker Rollin Soles of Argyle Winery explained to me his theories of growing Pinot Noir grapes. Good viticulture, according to Rollin, involves water management, plant density, crop control, and canopy management.

Water management—in other words, irrigation—is critical in farming. If the plants aren't getting enough water, they're not able to take full advantage of the heat and sunlight and will have limited capacity to produce excellent fruit. Argyle practices what's known as "deficit irrigation." If the vineyards hit a dry spell the objective is not to grow more leaves, but rather to maintain the leaves the plants already have. Even with a long dry spell, each plant receives a maximum of two gallons of water per year. Surprisingly, many neighboring vineyards are farming without any irrigation at all.

Plant density is critical to the process of photosynthesis. High leaf density is desirable because the more leaves, the more sun each plant catches, which in turn fuels the growth of the fruit.

At the same time, it's important to exercise crop control. The prevailing theory among the world's better winemakers is that it's unwise to ripen more than a certain percentage of fruit per acre. But Mother Nature doesn't know that. So Rollin and his team try to predict. They count grape clusters and try to project precisely the growth of the crop. This is accomplished by walking among the plants and literally counting the flower clusters in July, waiting until they bloom, and taking samples and weighing them in August. At that time Rollin decides how many clusters per plant should stay, and the rest are simply cut off. Usually, Argyle "drops" two-thirds of the grapes that are growing. If there are thirty clusters on a vine, Rollin and his crew will actually remove or drop twenty from the plant while the berries (this is how wine people refer to grapes) are still green so the ones that remain on the vine get all of the flavor.

Canopy management is the fourth critical element in viticulture. The plants and the fruit must get ample sunlight. Too much of a canopy (leaves) shading the fruit and the clusters won't get enough heat and light.

Rollin uses vines that are native to America and grafts European cuttings onto them. He selects root stocks that are devigorating—calculated to regulate the development of the vines in order to enhance their quality. There is much data analysis and observation involved in the selection and development of root stocks. Rollin will watch to see which vines are making big clusters, which are making small clusters, and what sorts of colors are developing. Depending upon the desired outcome, he might take cuttings from various plants and graft them to others.

The New World—and Oregon in particular—has a much shorter history of growing fine-wine grapes than Europe. What is being done in Oregon now may be totally discontinued in two generations, or it could be critical to the fu-

ture of viticulture. The choices today's Oregon winemakers make with respect to water management, plant density,
crop control, canopy management, and root stocks are experimental, and there's still much to learn. But that's also
what makes the process so exciting and why the wine gets
better every year.

For me as a restaurant customer, knowing what happens at the Argyle winery and vineyards alters my experience of drinking wine. I feel as though I have a relationship
with the product, and that when I drink it I'm participating in something bigger than just the here and now. Wine
is part of our history and culture, and Argyle is at the leading edge of risk taking, experimentation, and commitment
to quality. I take that in with every sip.

Most farmers and producers produce large quantities of
just a few things, and then try to sell them: Rollin Soles
produces his wines, Tony Blanchard harvests clams, and
Jonathan White makes his cheeses. But there is another
aspect of modern agriculture that affects restaurants:
custom-tailored production.

In British Columbia, in the Vancouver suburb of Surrey,
I meet farmers TJ and Ron Brar, brothers and owners of
Evergreen Herbs Ltd. Their production facility looks
nothing like a farm—it looks more like a university research laboratory. All employees wear lab coats and hair
nets and wash their shoes and hands with antibacterial
gels upon entering the facility. They pack herbs, baby let-
tuces, and vegetables under climate-controlled and air-
filtered conditions.

Behind the packing room, the Evergreen Herbs greenhouses stretch for nearly a mile. I feel a bit silly in my lab coat and hair net, in part because the coat is a size too small, but I soon forget as I lose myself in the diversity of the crops. Evergreen Herbs grows hundreds of varieties of vegetables, and within their abilities the Brars will grow just about anything a chef requests, and they'll grow it just for that chef. Any Vancouver-area chef, or any chef elsewhere willing to pay for shipping, can have Evergreen Herbs plant a predetermined area with a specific seed variety. This individualized approach to farming allows restaurants to have signature ingredients—green-and-yellow striped tomatoes, purple-and-white peppers, little-known herbs—that aren't the same as those used at every other restaurant in town.

Nearly everything is harvested to order, and the Evergreen Herbs people are no slouches in the early rising department: by 11 A.M. everybody goes home—they do all their picking and packing starting at 3 A.M. If a restaurant in Vancouver places an order with Evergreen in the evening, the herbs and baby vegetables will be hand-harvested early the next morning, packed, and delievered to the restaurant before lunchtime.

And when the deliveries are dropped off, there is always the gossip at the receiving dock: food purveyors are one of the restaurant industry's great reservoirs of information about what the other chefs in town are cooking, what new ingredients are coming down the pike, and, of course, who's sleeping with whom.

Most importantly, you can taste the Evergreen Herbs difference on the plate: such freshness creates almost the vegetable equivalent of sashimi.

•   •   •

From Tony Blanchard's clam farming operation to Rollin Soles's viticulture, and from Jonathan White's rustic cheese-making operation to the Brars' state-of-the-art production facility, science always informs agriculture. And at the scientific forefront today are several controversies of great importance to society: pesticides, organic farming, soil erosion, the protection of fisheries and habitats, the genetic modification of foods, mad-cow disease, and many other aspects of health and environmental safety. For each of these battlegrounds, there are articulate and principled people taking a variety of positions. I'm more concerned with the implications of what I see as a certain strain of risk-averseness of many regulators, organizations, chefs, and consumers. As governments work to restrict food choices through regulation, such as we've seen with cheese, a range of organizations, from the organically inclined Chefs Collaborative to the anti-globalization Slow Food movement, tend to shoot first and ask questions later when it comes to questions of the utility of science in agriculture, aquaculture, and food production and processing.

Organic foods, to take one example, hold tremendous appeal for some. There is little doubt that industrialization and the rise of agribusiness have harmed the flavor of many foods, elevating the needs of shipping and storage over what is good for the palate or the environment. But I think those who insist on only organic foods go too far. Used responsibly, pesticides and other modern agricultural methods are great assets to humanity—without them, we could not likely feed five billion people. Organic farming can yield beautiful produce, but ultimately great foods should be enjoyed no matter what technology was used to produce them. I've met many principled, excellent farmers and producers who apply modern technology with restraint to create artisanal-quality products that may not be organic, or that may rely on genetically modified clams, seeds, cultures, or vines, but that hardly run roughshod over the environment. Neither Niman Ranch nor Coleman Natural beef is organic—their owners support sustainable farming principles but don't believe it's necessary to demand, for example, that all the grain fed to their cattle be certified organic. I've also met cynical organic farmers who subscribe to organic certification programs solely so they can charge more money by selling their products to Whole Foods and boutique stores rather than regular supermarkets, and not because they believe in it. They treat organic certification processes the way creative accountants treat the tax code: they're mostly interested in finding the loopholes. I'd personally rather have a nonorganic apple that I picked myself in a nearby family-run Connecticut orchard (there is very little organic fruit production in the northeastern United States because the wet climate often requires the use of fungicides in order to grow fruit in a commercially viable manner) than an organic one from halfway around the world that has been sitting in the hold of a ship for a month, and where I'm not sure I trust the organic certification process anyway.

Beyond the governments and organizations, in America a general attitude of neopuritanism pushes against the hedonistic enjoyment of food. The message that indulging in food and drink, especially gourmet food and drink, is unhealthy, even sinful, is heard round the clock from the early morning fitness shows to the late night ads for weight-loss products. I also see, all too often, a general lack of adventurousness among Americans when it comes to trying new things.

To me, the farmers and producers who bring us wonderful foods are heroic. Whatever they grow, I want to eat: they inspire me to crave variety. Yet I have found that too many Americans have narrow taste horizons when it comes to trying new foods.

Most of us have expanded our taste horizons at least somewhat over the course of a life. But too many people reach a point, eventually, where they settle into a sensory routine: they like a few things, and they don't feel the need to acquire new tastes. This, to me, is a recipe for an unrewarding culinary life, or at least one that is less rewarding than it could be. And from a societal standpoint, it also guarantees boring restaurants that exhibit an alarming degree of sameness.

It is my hope, however, that by learning more about the origins of food we will all open our minds a bit more and look to broader culinary horizons. Try a taste of something you don't know or think you don't like, then try it again.

One thing I often thought as I visited farms was how disconnected we have become from our sources of food. The proverbial shrink-wrapped piece of meat in the Styrofoam supermarket tray hardly even seems like the product of any sort of natural process. At the same time, there is a certain brutality to the slaughter of animals that this disconnect seeks to shield us from.

In meeting so many farmers and their animals, however, I was never tempted to become a vegetarian. Every farmer I met eats his own animals; it is mostly in urban disconnected environments that people react to the meat-is-murder axiom by becoming vegetarians.

And there is certainly an extent to which meat is murder: the taking of a life. But the consumption and enjoyment of meat has a certain beauty of connectedness to it: it is a bridge between nature, farmers, our communities, and our traditions. Rather than teaching me to reject meat, the farmers of North America have taught me to respect it, to seek out superior products, and to value every bite.

Perhaps nothing captures the national pastime of feeling guilty about food, however, more than our obsession with diet, cholesterol, and weight loss. This is evident in everything from the "heart healthy" symbols on so many restaurant menus to the common practice of fibbing in order to portray restaurant food as less caloric or lower in fat than it is. "It has just a touch of cream." "It's just brushed with a little olive oil." "It has very little butter."

We've all heard the same lame jokes: "I'm going to schedule a quadruple bypass for right after dinner!" "I can feel my arteries hardening as I eat!" "I better go see my cardiologist tomorrow!" Everybody chuckles, but does anybody really think it's appropriate to joke about heart disease at the table, or anywhere else?

Still, people are merely parroting the message that is repeated constantly on television and is trumpeted by just about every newspaper and diet guru in America. Whether it is an attack on carbohydrates, calories, or fat, the message is always the same: food is bad for you.

Of course, food isn't bad for you. But worrying so much about food might be, according to some groundbreaking research by Dr. Paul Rozin of the University of Pennsylvania. Rozin, a psychology professor, has conducted a major cross-cultural study of food attitudes among more than one thousand Americans, French, Belgians, and Japanese. His research shows that, while the French overall associate eating with pleasure, Americans worry about food and associate it primarily with nutrition (the Belgians and Japanese come out statistically in the middle).

"There is a sense among many Americans that food is as much a poison as it is a nutrient, and that eating is almost as dangerous as not eating," says Rozin. For example, Americans are so freaked out about food that, when asked if they would be willing to give up eating altogether in favor of a pill that could fulfill all their nutritional needs, 26 percent said yes. This number actually strikes me as a little low, and would probably be higher if the cheese steak and Tastycake-loving population of Pennsylvania (the source of the U.S. data) were replaced with, say, the residents of Los Angeles. In any event, it was double the percentage of the French.

In addition, Rozin notes, "Americans try to categorize foods as good or bad, healthy or unhealthy. A third of Americans believe that salt and fat are toxic, like mercury. But most foods, salt and fat included, are healthy in moderation and become unhealthy only when consumed in excess. The French seem to have a better understanding of this notion of balance." And, Rozin suggests, France's attitude toward food may in part explain the superior health of the French.

Just about everybody has heard of the "French paradox," although most people incorrectly think it has something to do with red wine. But the French paradox properly defined is that, while only 4 percent of French people eat diets that meet U.S. nutritional guidelines, and while the French overall have higher levels of serum cholesterol than Americans, the incidence of heart disease in France is 33 percent lower than in America.

Not to be outdone by a real scientist, I once spent a month conducting a little psychological study of my own. One November, I dined in groups of three or more people on fourteen occasions (both at home and in restaurants). On thirteen occasions, people made one or more comments connecting the food with heart disease (twenty-two comments in all). In eleven cases, there were also comments about weight gain resulting from those meals (fifteen total comments). And one of those meals (three comments total) was at a vegetarian health food restaurant.

At only one group meal were there no comments about food and health. You guessed it, my dinner companions were French.

"The simple truth is that fat is delicious," says Edward Behr, editor of *The Art of Eating* quarterly newsletter. "Most of the flavor of meat comes from fat, and fat enriches the flavor of most any food. Fat carries flavor and feels luscious in the mouth. It's even delicious in certain raw forms, like olive oil and butter."

It's no wonder that, as Rozin puts it, "Every bite, for some people, is fraught with conflict." Exaggerated reporting of specious epidemiological studies (which only show correlations and do not offer explanations) has made us into a nation of hysterics. "This availability of information has not been accompanied by education of the public on risks and benefits, basic concepts of probability, and on the gradual and rocky road, in science, from ignorance to knowledge," he argues. "This has led, at least among Americans, to frequent new concerns about particular dietary items, and has promoted tendencies to ignore it all, or to overreact to it all, or to develop simplifying heuristics which take the uncertainty out of every bite."

But here's one thing we do know: stress is unhealthy. The studies showing links between stress and poor health are legion—Rozin will be happy to show you hundreds. And, as he concludes, "It is not unreasonable to assume that when a major aspect of life becomes stressful and a source of substantial worry as opposed to a pleasure, effects might be seen in both cardiovascular and immune systems."

In his movie *Sleeper* (1973), Woody Allen plays a man who, after years in cryogenic freeze, awakens in a future where superior science has established that cigarettes and chocolate are good for you and that, conversely, foods thought to be healthy in the twentieth century are actually carcinogenic. So the next time you find yourself face-to-face with a plate of creamy, salty, buttery mashed potatoes, or a medium-rare USDA Prime dry-aged steak, and especially a glass of pinot noir, enjoy them. Even better, ask for seconds. Your life may depend on it.

CHAPTER FOUR

The Restaurant Information Age

How many times have you been in this conversation:

"Where should we go for dinner?"

"Oh, anywhere you like. I don't really care."

"Okay, how about Italian?"

"No, I don't feel like Italian."

Add another person or two into the mix, and it gets even more complicated. In my experience, most people care very much where they dine and what they order, even (and perhaps especially) when they don't think they do. So what do you do if you're trying to pick a special restaurant for that important birthday or anniversary? Or if you're heading for a new town, or you're in one already, and you need a place to eat. How do you find the right restaurant?

Today we have an unprecedented amount of information available to us about everything, including restaurants. The challenge is not finding out about restaurants, but, rather, filtering out the noise and knowing which sources to trust.

It's worth weighing the value of and comparing information from those sources. Busy Americans, who may work ten or more hours a day (especially when factoring in the commute) and sleep seven or eight hours, may very well, after all other obligations are attended to, have only two or three hours of leisure time in a given day. A restaurant meal may occupy half or even all of that time. It may be the only opportunity of the day, or of the week, for busy parents to be alone together outside the bedroom. It is often our one opportunity to be served. And our enjoyment of dining is increased when we make intelligent, appropriate, and personally rewarding restaurant choices.

The most widely utilized restaurant information sources in America are the Zagat Surveys, the best-selling guides to restaurants in forty-five cities worldwide. Even at the most elite level, owners and chefs know that Zagat rankings are more important to success than the reviews of all the city's newspapers combined. Anyone who has availed himself of a Zagat Survey, with its narrow, elongated shape and distinctive red cover, will hardly be at a loss to explain its appeal. As a convenient and superbly organized guide, the Zagat Survey is unparalleled; with a new edition appearing every year, it is timely and comprehensive as well.

But are the Zagat Surveys a good way of rating restaurants? The fundamental premise of the Zagat Survey, as stated by Tim and Nina Zagat, the lawyers who started the company and built it into an international empire, is that "rating a restaurant on the basis of hundreds or even thousands of experiences [is] inherently more fair and accurate than relying on one reviewer and just a few meals." Stated this way, the notion appears reasonable enough: after all, at an average of 1,800 meals per restaurant surveyed, the 2000 guide for New York reflects no fewer than 3.2 million meals consumed. Surely that guarantees greater fairness and accuracy. Or does it?

It is a simple but distorting truth that people tend to prefer the restaurants they already frequent. The circular nature of this process has been well pinpointed by the critic Seymour Britchky: "Once you learn to hate a restaurant you never go back, [but] since you do not evaluate a restaurant for Zagat unless you have been there in the past year, those who continue to rate a place are, disproportionately, its admirers—fans—while the opinions of detractors go unrecorded." The former *New York Times* restaurant critic William Grimes has labeled this phenomenon "The Zagat Effect," adding that once a restaurant gets a good rating, "diners flock to it . . . and, convinced that they are eating at a top-flight establishment, cannot bring themselves to believe otherwise."

The scores and rankings in the Zagat Survey reflect, by definition, an average of the opinions gathered. But if you want to know how good a restaurant is, averages can be seriously misleading. An example of what can happen when one averages consumers with different levels of taste and (above all) experience was on display in the 1998–99 edition of Zagat's *America's Best Meal Deals*. On its nationwide list of "Top Delis," not a single New York delicatessen was to be found; instead, the guide featured places like d'Bronx Deli in Kansas City (which apparently doubles as a pizzeria) and another establishment in Salt Lake City.

It is as if the editors of *Consumer Reports* were to declare that their patient, meticulous, objective, and very expensive testing of air conditioners and washing machines actually resulted in a less accurate product guide than one based solely on the random and self-selected reports of buyers, whose opinions alone they would henceforth solicit.

It might also come as a surprise to anyone who has not participated in a Zagat Survey to learn that the 30-point ratings in the book do not represent actual choices. In fact, the survey form offers only four choices, 0 through 3. Thus, a conscientious participant who believes that a restaurant's rank should be, say, 25 on a 30-point scale must choose either a 2 or a 3, each of which represents an inaccurate extreme. These ratings are then averaged and multiplied to give the appearance of a more nuanced evaluation.

Another problem arises with time lag. As any professional critic can testify, accuracy in a restaurant review requires taking careful notes and then writing relatively quickly. After a few days, much specific recollection will be lost (this applies to music and dance reviews as well). But the Zagat Survey forms are mailed out once a year, with the specific intent that all restaurants be ranked at once and not necessarily in conjunction with actual meals. As with the simplified 4-point scale, this encourages impressionistic rankings at the extremes and, for places that have dramatically improved or dramatically deteriorated, the possibility of wholesale error.

Perhaps most surprising of all, respondents to the Zagat survey are not required to document—through, for example, copies of receipts—that they have actually eaten the meals they claim to be evaluating. The survey's voting controls consist only of computer programs that scan for major irregularities and discrepancies, which would hardly prevent a shut-in living in Bozeman, Montana, from voting in the Miami survey. Nor is there anything to prevent determined people from voting multiple times for their friends' restaurants, evaluating restaurants visited long ago or ranked according to the opinions of others, or engaging in conduct calculated to teach a restaurant a lesson—or make it number one. Online voting, recently introduced, will no doubt make it even easier to cast fictitious and/or ill-considered ballots.

There have been many consequences of this lack of safeguards. In the 1998 survey, for example, Ratner's restaurant on the Lower East Side of New York was described as offering "chicken soup that will cure anything short of amputations." Succinct, yes; accurate, no. Ratner's (a famous establishment that has since regrettably closed) was a kosher dairy restaurant and had never in its long history served a bowl of chicken soup.

None of which is to say the Zagat Survey is not useful. Like every other frequent diner in New York City, I keep one near me almost all the time: I have one in my minivan's glove compartment, one on my desk, and one I can't find right now. It's a great address and phone book, and it helps identify good places to eat in given neighborhoods and categories. But knowing what I know about the flaws in the methodology of the survey, what I read in Zagat I take with a grain of salt. Whatever Zagat says about a restaurant is one of many pieces of information available, valuable but neither infallible nor even terribly reliable.

The older European equivalent of Zagat—the Michelin Red Guide—comes at things from a different angle. The guide is published by the Michelin tire company as a side business that grew up with the early development of the French highway system. It rates restaurants on a scale from one to three stars. Being a "Michelin three-star restaurant" is possibly the highest accomplishment in the industry. There is also a rating system for unstarred restaurants that are nonetheless recommended. Even one Michelin star is a very high achievement—Europe, it seems, hasn't been gripped by grade inflation. Michelin publishes red guides to all the major destinations in Europe.

It's no surprise, then, that there has long been speculation about Michelin bringing its guidebook business to North America. And recently Michelin announced that it would be coming to New York in 2006, with other U.S. editions planned for later.

Will Michelin's arrival mean the end of Zagat's restaurant guidebook hegemony? I think the answer is no. America has long looked to Europe for culinary inspiration, but the same has not been true in culinary media. Zagat may not even be Michelin's real competition, because Michelin will have to compete with newspapers. Right now, for instance, when New Yorkers who know anything about fine dining speak of starred New York restaurants, they speak in terms of *New York Times* stars. They are the New York equivalents of Michelin stars in France, though the scales and systems are quite different: the *Times* uses a four-star scale, the requirements for receiving one star are not particularly high, and the whole orientation of the scale is toward New York's homegrown dining aesthetic. Several major American cities have local newspapers that use a four- or five-star restaurant rating system and have tremendous authority in the local market.

The question is, will Michelin be able to get its stars

recognized by the relevant upper-end of the consumer population, or will the Michelin stars just be a curiosity to New Yorkers and those in the other cities into which Michelin might expand? My sense is that Michelin will, and should, fail to gain traction in the United States.

For starters, the Michelin system is ill-suited to a polyglot dining culture. It has barely even been sustainable, from a consistency standpoint, since the nouvelle cuisine era in France. (In France, Michelin has remained strong thanks to substantial momentum accumulated during decades of supremacy, but it has no such clout here.) Many Americans know about Michelin stars in Europe, but what percentage of Americans who have been to Michelin-starred restaurants in France have actually bothered to buy a Michelin guide, or have ever even seen the pages of one? The consensus of educated observers seems to be that overall Michelin yields the best ratings for France, where every relevant restaurant is French and where the fine-dining restaurants have some sort of intuitive or perhaps explicit understanding of the items on the Michelin checklist, which they pursue aggressively in order to achieve star rankings.

Michelin's ratings of restaurants in New York, which will be its first step toward what Michelin hopes will be a series of American regional guides, if performed with the same set of assumptions probably won't seem relevant to anyone outside of France. America is significantly more "foreign" to France than any of the countries that are now covered by the guides. And at a time when the top French chefs are looking to America for inspiration, it seems particularly bizarre to have a French ranking system attempt to enter this market. This presents a conundrum for

Michelin: either use the French system and generate out-of-context ratings, or hire American inspectors and editors to create an American system and lose the cachet of the Michelin system.

The category of high-volume high-energy fine dining doesn't really exist in France, other than in places that are direct responses to American restaurants (such as Alain Ducasse's Spoon and Joel Robuchon's Atelier). New York, which is emblematic of the urban American dining culture, is a different universe. Michelin's stars, in that sense, miss the point: New York restaurants simply haven't oriented themsleves toward the pursuit of Michelin stars. While places like Alain Ducasse New York and Per Se are super-luxe and slow-paced, like the three-stars in France, they're not fundamentally part of the home-grown New York scene. The *New York Times* system, though it has been diluted by a succession of critics who have been sloppy with their stars, is the better way to represent New York restaurants on their own terms. It's a system appropriate to the market and understood by people in the market.

Then there is the matter of the Michelin methodology. For years, Michelin enjoyed an aura of infallibility and scientific rigor. The widespread belief was that Michelin's expert, unimpeachable, anonymous inspectors fanned out across the European landscape, frequently visiting restaurants and judging them according to clear (albeit secret) criteria. But recent revelations by a disgruntled inspector have been disastrous for Michelin's credibility. In his *L'inspecteur se met à Table (The Inspector Sits at the Table)*, former Michelin inspector Pascal Rémy tells of a Michelin organization that is highly political, whose inspectors don't visit the restaurants very often, and that relies mostly on an impressionistic system. Remy claims that at least a third of Michelin three-star restaurants are not up to snuff, that there is a whole class of politically immune restaurants with star ratings that are inviolate, and that the guide's editors are easily influenced by pressure such as letter-writing campaigns. Michelin comes out looking much more like an electing-the-pope system, where a bunch of cardinals sit in a room and hold secret discussions until the smoke signal goes up.

Michelin does not, after all, review restaurants. It is purely a rating system—there is virtually no critical text in the guides. Whatever substantive comments might be made based on the inspection visits are kept secret. European audiences have traditionally been willing to accept that. Some Americans with a when-in-Rome attitude accept it in Europe as well. I find it hard to believe, however, that Americans will accept that method with respect to their restaurants, when there is such an information-rich food media already in place. Maybe if the inspectors were known to the public and eminently qualified, maybe if the comments were expanded to include actual reasoning, maybe if Michelin could create a perception that it has embraced the local restaurant scene on its own terms . . . maybe under those circumstances the guide could enter the market with an enthusiastic reception. But that would involve Michelin rejecting all the fundamental elements of its system.

At the same time, with their shortcomings in mind, it is certainly possible to benefit from the Michelin and Zagat guides. Over time, comparing meals you've enjoyed to the restaurants recommended by the guides, you'll be able to start predicting which kinds of comments and ratings appeal to your tastes. For example, you may find that Zagat's recommendations are reliable when it comes to small neighborhood places but not with respect to fine dining, and that Michelin has the opposite strengths and weaknesses.

There is a larger question, though: do we even benefit from stars and numeric rankings of restaurants? Such rankings imply a level of objectivity that is unattainable when reviewing restaurants. Looking through the *New York Times*, I see no stars or scores accompanying the film, art, architecture, and music reviews, and critics at some other papers who assign scores to such subjects run the risk of trivializing the arts criticism aspect of their work. So why try to quantify restaurants, especially in a nation where chefs eschew conformity in favor of creativity?

I prefer to hear about a restaurant (or a wine, or a concert) not in numbers, codes, or stars, but in plain English. And knowledgeable diners are looking for exactly what both Michelin and Zagat have never and will never offer: reviews with substance. It would seem, then, that the best source for restaurant information would be the professionally written reviews that appear in newspapers and magazines. But these reviews, and the reviewers who write them, also are not infallible. A full-length restaurant review by a single named author may be inherently superior to a capsule review by an anonymous group, if only because it offers detail and accountability. But the informed consumer must read restaurant criticism with a critical eye.

Part of the problem with many restaurant reviewers today, especially those at the larger metropolitan and national publications, is that they position themselves in opposition to restaurants. This would be self-defeating in most forms of criticism: imagine an art critic who is fundamentally anti-artists, or a film critic who dislikes directors, actors, and studios. Yet the highest-profile restaurant reviewers have cultivated a reputation for anti-restaurant behavior that crosses the line between standard journalistic skepticism and ritualized mistrust. They avoid chefs, restaurateurs, and especially publicists like the plague—at least they tell the public they do—and they make a big show of dining anonymously in the hopes of catching sneaky restaurateurs trying to foist bad food and service on an unsuspecting public. Ruth Reichl and Mimi Sheraton, former *New York Times* critics, were famous for wearing wigs in order to disguise their identities. Those wigs sometimes were even sold at charity auctions. *Saveur* magazine titled an article I wrote about Mimi Sheraton and the restaurateur Sirio Maccioni of Le Cirque "The Critic and Her Prey."

But did those wigs actually make them anonymous, and more importantly is anonymity and distance from the industry really the be-all-end-all of restaurant reviewing? I prefer to think that the way to improve the state of fine dining in America is to bring consumers and the industry closer together—that is one of my aims in this book—and thus I have long felt that the emphasis on anonymity and distance in restaurant reviewing establishes a poor dynamic between those constituencies. It sends a signal to the public that restaurants are out to deceive us, and that in order to expose them restaurant reviewers must act as undercover investigative consumer advocates.

In my experience, most people in the restaurant business aren't trying to rip us off but are, rather, trying to do a good job and provide good value to customers. In many cases, we get better restaurants than we deserve. Most customers would settle for less, and are brought along to a higher standard by the vision of a small group of true believers in the restaurant business. There's an element of idealism in opening any restaurant above the level of a McDonald's. Most of the better restaurateurs I've met are smart and savvy enough to make a lot more money as lawyers or investment bankers. They choose food because they love it, not because they want to steal our money.

But one has to wonder what the deeper motivation is for this focus on a strict division between reviewers and the industry. In part, it is surely an attempt to assure the public that the critics are impartial, like any kind of journalist. But I think it goes beyond that: journalistic detachment and independence are one thing, but the wigs and suspicion pander to and reinforce a public perception that restaurants are inherently dishonest. Consumer protection is important, but the consumer protection function of reviews has today overwhelmed the potentially valuable content that could be delivered in reviews.

As any reporter will tell you, there is simply no substitute for in-person interaction. And personal relationships get you more information. Any critic who tells you he can get as much information out of a chef on the phone as he can by spending time in his kitchen is delusional. If a food writer goes to an industry dinner event and sits next to a restaurateur, he's going to learn more than during any phone conversation. And if the restaurateur knows the writer personally and trusts that he's a responsible and competent writer and won't misreport what the restaurateur says, he will be even more open. Moreover, because they have history, the reporter knows he can trust the restaurateur—something that is unfortunately not the case with respect to most chefs and restaurateurs. Surely, that trust can be abused—it is always a fragile thing—but that's the world of journalism.

There is, to my mind, absolutely nothing wrong with a critic having ties—close ties—to the community about which he writes. In my opinion, it is preferable from the standpoint of providing the best possible coverage. To me, the primary function of restaurant criticism should not be something so prosaic as reporting on the average meal and labeling it with some stars. Rather, restaurant criticism should parallel other forms of criticism—in art, literature, architecture, and music—such that critics are champions of excellence who promote the best within the industry while exposing the worst. And my hope is that after reading this book, you won't be eating average meals.

A good review should teach something. A good review should increase the reader's knowledge of the restaurant and of dining in general in ways that do not limit themselves by the consumer protection elements of the review. It couldn't be clearer to me that the cloistered restaurant reviewer is inadequate to this task. It may be possible to conduct some follow-up interviews on the phone, but there are other ways to maintain detachment while still gathering a lot of information in person. Anybody who thinks he can get all the best information without directly engaging chefs and restaurateurs up close and personally is like a sports writer never interviewing a coach or entering the locker room.

Moreover, it is quite impossible for the most influential newspaper reviewers in major markets to remain anonymous. And this raises an issue too. Only the insignificant restaurants, or the ones that slip up, will fail to recognize a critic and therefore receive truly anonymous reviews. As a critic for the *New York Times*, you will never make it through the front door of Le Cirque 2000 without being recognized. Even if you have plastic surgery in anticipation of the review, the scrub nurse will have sold photos of your new likeness to Sirio Maccioni, Le Cirque's owner, before you cross the threshold.

But what about special treatment for critics? Surely, a recognized critic will get special food and service and therefore can not write an objective review.

The treatment a recognized critic receives is, certainly, better than that afforded a stranger to a restaurant. But it is unlikely to be too far removed from the baseline. As former *New York Times* critic Bryan Miller, who had worked in a French restaurant kitchen when several known critics came in, observes, "When the owners told us what was happening I realized there was little we could do. By this time all our sauce stocks had been prepared, the fish, meat, and vegetables purchased, and the desserts made." He concludes, "On any given day, a kitchen can perform only up to its level of competence (or incompetence, as the case may be); nothing magical can be done for a critic's sake."

So, if he is recognized, a critic's plates will receive extra special attention in the kitchen, guaranteeing that they represent the restaurant at its best. And that critic surely will be assigned the restaurant's best servers. In other words, he will receive the treatment that a highly valued VIP customer receives.

As I hope you will learn from reading this book, it is just about the easiest thing in the world to become a regular at any restaurant and to start receiving the best treatment on your first visit. So for those of you who have read this book, shouldn't reviews tell us which restaurants we might want to be regulars at, and why? And how can that story—the real story of any restaurant—be told from the perspective of the anonymous outsider?

Veteran critics are also, for the most part, neither stupid nor naive. They can usually tell when a restaurant is putting on a show for them, and they can compensate for that when trying to evaluate the performance of the kitchen and waitstaff. They can monitor other tables and talk to trusted confederates with whom they dine often and whose opinions they rely on as a reality check. They are not so easily fooled.

There is another aspect to restaurant reviews as well: entertainment. And of course, those who write well implicitly aim to entertain. But it is unfortunate that today there are many restaurant reviewers who have gone on record saying their job is to sell papers. This is particularly true in the United Kingdom, but it is also a problem here in the United States.

One of the foremost practitioners of shocking restaurant reviewing is the British restaurant reviewer A. A. Gill, who has also written New York restaurant reviews for *Vanity Fair*. His self-conscious outrageousness led him to write of Jean-Georges Vongerichten's restaurant 66: "How clever are shrimp-and-foie-gras dumplings with grapefruit dipping sauce? What if we called them fishy liver-filled condoms? They were properly vile, with a savor that lingered like a lovelorn drunk and tasted as if your mouth had been used as the swab bin in an animal hospital." Describing the rest of the meal: "The memory of the rest has been elided into one long, bland, watery compost that could barely incite flatulence."

In my opinion, that kind of "criticism" is beneath contempt. There's a point at which exaggeration for dramatic effect borders on unfair. Gill should not be squandering his talent in such an undignified manner. And it's not as though this was a one-time slip-up or a reaction to one particularly vile dish. Rather, this sort of writing is Gill's modus operandi as a food writer. His "Table Talk" column in the *Sunday Times* of London has offered, among others, a description of one restaurant's risotto as having "cleverly and precisely contrived the three Ts—taste, texture, and temperature—of happy, youthful vomit" and of another restaurant's dessert as a "clungy, sputoid vanilla slice that was like eating sweet Magimixed maggots." As reported by Warren St. John in the *New York Times*, Gill is "the unofficial ringleader of a pack of sometimes hilarious, astonishingly brutal restaurant critics who in the last few years have turned English food writing into a blood sport."

As the Association of Food Journalists says in its critics guidelines (with which I take issue on several other points, but not this one): "Good restaurant reviewing is good journalism. Reviewers should subscribe to the same accepted standards of professional responsibility as other journalists." A critic has a particularly heavy journalistic burden, because it's so easy to use the "it's my opinion" excuse to justify any behavior. But a critic has an obligation to base opinions on information, to render professional rather than personal opinions (a personal relationship with a chef or restaurateur should give a critic better information and insight, but should not affect conclusions about the quality of the establishment), and moreover to communicate his or her true opinions rather than opinions designed to sell more papers. Critics have tremendous power, and any critic who doesn't view that power as a serious responsibility is a failure as a journalist.

The failings of some critics became painfully apparent back in 2001, when Alain Ducasse, considered by most serious observers to be the world's preeminent French chef, announced that he would be opening a restaurant in New York's Essex House hotel. It was to be the most expensive American restaurant ever, with set menus at $160 per person. By the time the 65-seat restaurant lit its stoves in late June, it had amassed a waiting list of 2,700 names—many of them customers of Ducasse's restaurants in Europe—and was the most sought-after reservation in the history of New York.

Then the reviews started coming in. First, then–*New York Times* critic William Grimes, in a "preview" of the restaurant after one visit, spoke deprecatingly of the high prices and the difficulty of securing a reservation (a reservation I had secured for him, rather easily, by hitting redial a few times on my phone). His praise for the food was faint, while with regard to everything else he maintained an attitude of detached amusement, withholding final judgment until he would have a chance to return more than once in the future.

Grimes's decorum gave way, in the *New York Post*'s Steve Cuozzo, to anger. Calling ADNY "the most arrogantly launched eatery in the history of the world," Cuozzo wrote scathingly that "globe-girdling Alain Ducasse means to tap Manhattan's cash gusher while it lasts, and ADNY is the mediocre, often comical result." He dismissed the luxury appointments as "gimmickry," the food as "middle-of-the-road classic."

This same theme was echoed in scores of other media outlets. Ducasse was lambasted for arrogance and French-style culinary imperialism; for exhibiting a corporate mentality, manifested above all in his frequent absences from ADNY itself; for the pretentiousness of his restaurant's appointments; for those prices; and, finally, for ADNY's allegedly unremarkable food. When I dined at ADNY, however, I found the food and service to be wonderful, and while there can always be debate about the virtues of a given dish, it seemed undeniable to me that ADNY is fundamentally a great restaurant.

It was at this time that I first realized there was something very wrong with the community of food critics in New York (from which, for better or worse, the rest of American food media largely take their cues). As I sought to understand the hostility that gave rise to these reviews of ADNY, I started to see a pattern: the reviewing business had lost sight of its mission. Or, perhaps, it never had a mission in the first place. After all, when the world's top chef opens a restaurant in New York City only to be met by a critical chorus of Bronx cheers, something is clearly going on.

To understand the problems with the critics, it is necessary to understand the flaws with their arguments. For example, from whence did the charge of arrogance against Ducasse derive? To me, it never made sense. There is little debate that Alain Ducasse is, in fact, the world's number one chef (the only serious competition for this title would be from the avant-garde master Ferran Adria, in Spain), or that he is currently at the top of his form. In a nutshell, he is the only chef of our generation to operate simultaneously two restaurants that have earned three Michelin stars (the highest accolade available in European restaurant ratings), while another two of his establishments—he had eleven altogether at the time of the reviews—boast one star apiece, making him history's only eight-star chef, and counting.

Given his success, nobody could fault him for displaying a high degree of self-confidence. But arrogance? Cultural imperialism? Ducasse has called New York "undoubtedly the most spectacular restaurant city due to its synthesis of international cultures"—no small compliment from a Michelin three-star chef. He is also passionate about American ingredients and has written an entire book, *Harvesting Excellence*, on the subject. If his desire to meld the best of French technique with the best of American ingredients constitutes arrogance, it is arrogance of a most peculiar sort. By all accounts, Ducasse is one of the hardest-working chefs in history. He could easily rest on his laurels; with eight Michelin stars to his credit, it may be a century before anyone achieves a comparable level of eminence. He also had little to gain and much to lose by opening a place in New York, a notorious snakepit for restaurateurs with grand designs. What the critics missed, though this reality was staring them in the faces the whole time, is that it was not arrogance but rather idealism, in the form of a lifelong commitment to the cause of fine dining—as well, of course, as the ambition to succeed—that led Ducasse into this venture.

That the media felt Ducasse was arrogant for trying to be excellent was, perhaps, a sign of the times. It also represented, no doubt, a species of xenophobia and resentment: who is this French guy to tell us what defines excellence in dining? (He's the world's greatest chef, is who he is.) And there is a dirty little secret beyond all this: Ducasse failed to manage and manipulate the media as successfully as some others. He didn't play the PR game well. He didn't throw the lavish pre-opening parties that were de rigueur among his American colleagues. He didn't offer priority reservations to journalists—they had to wait on line and on hold like everybody else. It seems clear, in retrospect, that there was an element of teaching-Ducasse-a-lesson in the media responses.

When I was struggling to explain the critics' behavior at the time, a friend described this behavior as "the critics pandering to the peanut gallery." But I came to realize it was something worse: the critics had become the peanut gallery.

In the days when the late Craig Claiborne was at the *New York Times*, restaurant reviewers were culled from the ranks of trained culinary professionals and self-educated gourmets. Today, they are more likely to be journalists doing a job. As William Grimes candidly described his own qualifications, "I'm an amateur eater who's turned pro." To his credit, Grimes generally acquitted himself pretty well. The same unfortunately cannot be said for the performance of his successor, Frank Bruni, another company man new to restaurant criticism. Bruni, the former film critic for the *Detriot Free Press* and the author of the book *Ambling into History: The Unlikely Odyssey of George W. Bush*, wrote more than 1,000 articles for the *New York Times* before becoming the restaurant critic. They include hundreds of stories about the 2000 presidential campaign, New York metro happenings, and reports during his stint as Rome bureau chief. But he wrote only a handful of stories containing any discussion of food. His restaurant reviews reflect his limited experience, expertise, and perspective, as well as a preoccupation with issues other than food. When he demoted the restaurant Bouley from four stars (the highest available ranking from the *Times*) to three, he seemed as determined to discuss gossip about the chef as he was to discuss the food, and while the restaurant had been operating since 1987 he had never before visited ("I had the sense of being at a party to which I had come too late," he wrote). In his first four-star review, of the restaurant Per Se, he added little to what other critics had already written. He devoted a review to comparing two steakhouses, Wolfgang's and Peter Luger, and wrote more about cardiology and his night on the town with a friend than about the meat. On election night 2004, he was not out expanding his culinary horizons but was, rather, writing "An Election Night Web Journal" for NYTimes.com.

If the critics can be wrong about the best restaurants, they can be wrong about any restaurant. It is terribly disappointing to me when I recommend a restaurant I know someone will like and that person says, "But it wasn't well reviewed." Maybe not, but as with Zagat and Michelin, one should remember to look at restaurant reviews as opinions. In the end, that's what they are. Moreover, they are opinions targeted at a wide audience, not at a given person's tastes and preferences. When reading restaurant reviews, don't let a claim like "the beef was nearly raw" go unchallenged. You may prefer your beef that way.

• • •

So if neither Zagat, Michelin, nor the critics provide enough reliable information about restaurants, where can we turn? Is there another way?

I think there is. It's called the Internet.

The Internet, by eliminating the costs associated with publishing, allows two primary species of content: that which isn't good enough for print, and that which doesn't fit into the architecture of any particular print journal either because it's too offbeat or too hot for print to handle (low-budget online media are less risk-averse, especially when it comes to defamation law, than print). Online publishing also eliminates concerns of length, thus allowing for more detail (or, sometimes, less discipline). Even publishing work that is not particularly well written is sometimes a virtue, however, as it allows new voices to develop and new ideas to be propagated regardless of writing skill, just as theoretically in a courtroom the best arguments and not the most eloquent lawyers should triumph.

Online writing has another benefit: it is largely immune to the incestuousness of the food magazines and newspaper food sections. When is the last time, for example, that you saw any serious criticism of one food magazine in another food magazine—an editorial in *Gourmet* disagreeing with something in *Saveur*? Has any major newspaper restaurant critic ever taken on another newspaper restaurant critic in a review? There is a code of silence in these print media; other publications barely exist. Not so online, where media watchdogs of all stripes prosper, even in the relatively tame food arena.

But writing of the traditional sort—the article, the

essay—is only the most basic species of online content. The Internet has given rise to new forms, ones that don't and can't exist in print, yet offer an amazing depth and diversity of content. One such phenomenon is what is called "blogging." Not a pretty name, but a great phenomenon: a blog, which is short for Weblog, is a cross between a magazine article series and a personal diary. It allows a writer to communicate directly with readers on a daily basis, with a focus on events as they unfold. For example, one might see a daily blog by a writer traveling across the United States, or Europe, or Africa, or Mongolia. With the availability of handheld digital cameras and Internet hookups most everywhere, readers can receive daily dispatches. There are also opinion blogs, photo blogs, and even blogs that just follow a person's daily life. Of course, blogging is well suited to coverage of dining—there are pizza blogs, burger blogs, and food-travel blogs aplenty—as well as cooking, food media and literature, and even chronicles of attendance at culinary school. Not all of these blogs are interesting, but many are. And no newspaper or magazine would ever support such an activity—at most one would see a heavily produced, stripped-down weekly series that glosses over all the detail and spontaneity that make blogs so special. Most importantly, anybody can be a blogger. The technology is now as simple to use as AOL or MSN (if you know what either of those things is, you can be a blogger). There are now free and low-cost blogging services that do all the work for you. All the blogger needs to do is type and click.

The most important contribution of the Internet has not been the Webzine or the Weblog but, rather, the Web community. A Web community takes writing to the next level, by making it interactive. Everybody in the community is at once an author and a reader, and their writings and interpretations interact synergistically so as to be more than the sum of their parts. If you've never participated in a Web community discussion, it can be disorienting at first. There are "threads" of discussion and "posts" by individuals within those threads. There can be "categories," "forums," and "sub-forums" to further categorize and subdivide the discussions. But in the end it is simply a conversation, somewhat like a roundtable or panel discussion, where people take turns speaking on a given subject—and sometimes many subjects. At the same time, Web communities allow people with specific interests to come together despite geographic separation.

It was this vision that led me and my colleague Jason Perlow to found the eGullet Web community in August of 2001. I had been writing on my own blog site, Fat-Guy.com, for four years and was feeling that the site had peaked. In particular, I was concerned that the heavy regional orientation of Fat-Guy.com, which was mostly a site about a New Yorker and restaurants in New York, was ultimately self-limiting. I noticed that several of my online food-blogging colleagues—like Matthew Amster-Burton in Seattle and Andy Lynes in the United Kingdom—were in a similar bind. We were also facing stiff competition from nationwide ventures like Sidewalk.com (a now-defunct national cityguide site created by Microsoft) and CitySearch.com (which performed the same function and later swallowed up Sidewalk.com). For example, I found that many New Yorkers knew to turn to Fat-Guy.com for New York restaurant recommendations, and I was proud that many savvy diners trusted my recommendations over those of the major newspaper critics. Likewise, there were many in Seattle who trusted Matthew Amster-Burton in the same way. Yet nobody in Seattle knew to come to Fat-Guy.com for New York recommendations—they only knew to go to CitySearch or to the Web site of a newspaper like the *New York Times*.

At the same time, I was coming to the point where I wanted to do more than just review restaurants. I wanted to help people understand how to dine, and work to improve food media in general, both online and in print. The answer, it seemed clear, was to bring independent food blog sites in various cities around the world together in a community.

Jason Perlow, a computer systems integration expert and senior technology editor at *Linux Magazine* (and also a devout foodie) had been my good friend for several years at this point (we met online), and had helped me redesign the Fat-Guy.com site. He believed strongly that the best community-building technologies available simply were not being utilized by anybody in the food realm. He had a broader vision for our affiliation of sites: he wanted a full-blown interactive community, including discussion forums, blogs, original articles and essays, recipes, photographs, book reviews . . . at the time it seemed such a grand over-the-top vision that nobody took it seriously except for Jason.

Jason, however, had the last laugh. Today, eGullet is a veritable nexus of the global food scene, with an audience of professional chefs and amateur cooks, restaurant consumers and artisanal food producers, amateur writers and the food media elite. What was eGullet.com became eGullet.org, the eGullet Society for Culinary Arts & Letters, a not-for-profit public service organization with a mission of "increasing awareness and knowledge of the arts of cooking, eating and drinking, as well as the literature of food and drink." I'm now the executive director, and Jason is on the board of trustees.

There are two things I like most about the restaurant discussions online as opposed to those in print. First, online you can interact directly with like-minded people. And in any online community, once you get to know the players, you learn quickly whom to trust. I have found in the past few years that, restaurant for restaurant, the online communities focus on the brass-tacks culinary issues—are the food and service good?—more often than the agenda-laden professional critics. Moreover, many of the best professional food writers these days are members of online communities, so their voices get added to the mix. While there is always a danger of dilution and the distraction of too many voices, a careful reader of online culinary discussions can cut through the agendas and the biases to get to the bottom of things rather quickly.

Second, while print media are solely focused on where to eat, online discussions also contain a wealth of information on how to dine. Every restaurant, as I've said, is really two restaurants: the one for the tourists, and the one where the regulars eat. Throughout the online discussions, you will find information on how to make the most of specific restaurants, and every restaurant, so as to get the treatment regulars get even on your first visit. To that extent, online media pick up where print media leave off.

All media, print and online, need to get their information from somewhere. The dining media get much of their information from eating at restaurants, but they also need to find out about those restaurants in the first place. In the proverbial small town of old, a restaurant solely dedicated to serving casual meals to the local population could conceivably just open its doors for business and hope to build a clientele rather quickly. But in most of America today, if a new restaurant opens without the benefit of any publicity, advertising, media coverage, or word-of-mouth buzz, it will be like the proverbial tree that falls in the forest but nobody hears. How do we learn about restaurants before they open, so that when they open there are customers to fill the seats and reviewers to write reviews?

The first time I ever received an e-mail from a restaurant publicist, my first thought was, "There's such a thing as a restaurant publicist?" Having spent most of my life as a restaurant consumer, I had never realized how much went on behind the scenes to bring restaurant information to me. That's because the business of disseminating restaurant information to the consumer goes mostly unnoticed. Those who perform these tasks are facilitators, not ends in themselves. But without them, restaurants couldn't succeed, and promoting restaurants is big business.

The publicity and advertising industries are heavily occupied with food, and some agencies handle restaurant clients only. Most major metropolitan newspapers have an entire weekly section devoted to food. The Zagat Surveys are a $100 million international business. And in casual conversation and on the Internet, restaurants are one of the hot topics of conversation, right up there with real estate, mutual funds, and the latest Hollywood movies.

It wasn't always this way. Half a century ago, the answer to the question "There's such a thing as a restaurant publicist?" would have been "no." There were press agents who could promote a party, but the modern concept of the restaurant publicist wasn't part of the equation. It took a man named Roger Martin to change all that.

Roger Martin, among other things, came up with the name Windows on the World when the famous restaurant in the World Trade Center was being planned in the 1970s. He had started his restaurant career in the 1950s working the coat check at the "21" Club while studying at New York University, and he joined up with one of the twentieth century's great restaurateurs, Joe Baum, in 1959. At Baum's company, Restaurant Associates, Roger Martin was responsible for opening many of the most famous restaurants in New York, including the Four Seasons. In 1979, after operating his own restaurant on Long Island for several years and overseeing the opening of Windows on the World, he decided to parlay his knowledge of restaurant openings, his media contacts, and his considerable personality into a new business: a restaurant consulting and public relations firm.

Not that I knew any of this when I started my food writing career. The first e-mail I ever got from Roger Martin, triggered by his happening upon a hamburger article I wrote on the Internet, just said: "ON BURGERS YOU HAVE MISSED TWO OF THE BEST: BALTHAZAR AND CITY HALL." (In online parlance, writing in all capitals is known as "shouting.") The message contained no identifying information other than his name. I filed it away for future reference. As he became more familiar with my work, however, his messages got longer and more detailed. The one time we ever met, over the aforementioned burger at the restaurant City Hall, he noted that he did consulting and publicity work for restaurants, but I never followed up. It wasn't until a year or so later, after he and I were well into an e-mail friendship, that another publicist mentioned to me, "You know Roger Martin invented the whole restaurant consulting and PR profession, right?"

Roger Martin and I exchanged nearly five hundred e-mail messages between the first time he contacted me and the last time I heard from him just a couple of months before his death. I never truly dealt with him in his capacity as a publicist—by then he was in his late sixties and basically retired. Rather, I knew him as a man who cared passionately about food, who took an interest in my writing for no other reason than that he knew he could help (after his death I learned from many people that Roger had promoted me behind the scenes, quietly and selflessly getting my name out to key players in the industry and the press), who forced me to think, who spoke with incredible authority and depth of experience, and who turned me on to a number of restaurant finds.

Having received countless invitations from publicists in the past, I decided when researching this book to turn the tables: I invited four of the publicists I respect most to my house for dinner, in order to learn more about this underappreciated and often misunderstood area of the business.

My guests for the evening were Shelley Clark of Lou Hammond Associates, Jennifer Baum of Bullfrog & Baum, and Karen Diaz and Frank Schloss of Diaz*Schloss. Shelley Clark specializes in hotel and corporate restaurants (she represents Tavern on the Green, for example, as well as the restaurants at hotels like the Waldorf=Astoria), Jennifer Baum represents some of the hottest properties in town (such as David Burke's restaurant davidburke & do-natella; she is also the daughter-in-law of Roger Martin's mentor, Joe Baum), and Karen Diaz and Frank Schloss are a husband-and-wife team operating a boutique PR firm out of New Jersey, with a lengthy roster of low-key, high-end restaurant clients like the midtown restaurant Beacon and the legendary bartender Dale "King of Cocktails" DeGroff.

One thing that's easy is getting publicists to talk.

The best publicists have a simple secret. As Shelley Clark puts it, "they don't take on any bad clients." They know it takes years to build up a relationship with any serious food media person (writer, editor, or television producer), but it only takes one bad pitch to wreck that relationship. They know that above all else a good product has to be a good product, and that the role of the publicist isn't to sell crap to the media but, rather, to present a good product in the best possible light.

"The most awkward part of the business," says Frank Schloss, "is giving a potential client an honest assessment of potential. Oftentimes we're called in to a new restaurant, we meet the management team, and we schedule a tasting . . . and the food turns out to be mediocre. That's when we have to stare the owner in the face and say, you know what? Every parent thinks his baby is the cutest on the block, but you've got an ugly baby. Because if they don't hear it from us, they're going to hear it in the press."

More importantly, the best publicists understand that media relations is only one facet of the PR business. What I found in talking to them is that they see themselves as members of a series of overlapping partnerships: with their chef and restaurateur clients (as well as producers of gourmet products), with the public, with members of the press, and with the overall progress of the restaurant industry. Collectively, they represent an invisible guiding force behind many trends and success stories.

A good publicist is involved in everything from letterhead design and customer comment cards, to menu development and newsletter mailings, to reservations policies and selection of waitstaff uniforms, to the restaurant's music mix and tableware choices. It is now almost unheard of for a successful high-end restaurant to function without someone dedicated to the task of public relations; if it's not a publicist at a PR firm, it will likely be someone on the restaurant's staff.

To the extent publicists help restaurants to communicate, they are a helpful source of information for the restaurant consumer, but most consumers never get to see the press releases. And press releases are self-serving—they are not independent, critical documents. Many restaurants and PR firms, however, place their press releases right on their Web sites, and they often make for interesting reading. It's especially fun to compare press releases to the language in newspaper and magazine food sections, in order to see how much influence the publicists really have. As on many corporate Web sites, there is often more to be learned in the press section, usually hidden away behind a faint link at the margins of the home page, than in the main part of the site.

The restaurant customer who reads guidebooks, newspapers, magazines, online sources, and restaurant PR materials together will be better off for it. This sounds like a daunting task, but think of purchasing a television or other consumer product that costs a few hundred dollars. For those to whom a few hundred dollars means something, it's worth the time to check in with *Consumer Reports*, various online sources, and knowledgeable friends before buying a piece of equipment. A restaurant meal can easily cost a few hundred dollars as well, and once you get into the routine of checking multiple sources (bookmarks in your Web browser; a little stack of guidebooks in a convenient place) it only takes a few minutes to gather the information needed to avoid a lousy meal or zero in on a great one.

But before guidebooks, reviews, the Web, and the words of publicists and news sources even enter the picture, let me suggest that there are two primary sources worth looking to: your own preferences and a restaurant's menu.

Understanding one's own preferences and needs, as well as those of your dining companions, is foundational to making good restaurant choices. When I meet new people and they learn I'm a restaurant critic, the first thing they say (after "Really? I've never heard of you") is "What's your favorite restaurant?" I have answers about what my favorites are, but would much rather help people connect with their favorite restaurants than tell them mine. If I can find out which restaurants and styles of dining they already like and dislike, I'm in a much better position to recommend new favorites to them. As in dating, not every restaurant is for every person. A restaurant may be good, but that doesn't mean you have to like it. Moreover, I don't want to dine at my favorite restaurants every night. Sometimes, and especially after several fancy meals in a row, I feel overstimulated and I just want a hamburger.

Finding the best restaurant for you is about finding the

best fit at a given place and time. And a large part of that fit has to do with whether or not you're in that restaurant's target audience. Are you what's called, sometimes derogatorily, a "foodie"? If so, your dining experiences and choices will mostly be dictated by food. But even foodies care about service, decor, ambience, noise, crowds, the space between tables, price, the time commitment of a given meal, location, and, most of all, they *should* care about the needs of their dining companions. We rarely dine alone in restaurants (although it can be the best way to experience cuisine), so most every restaurant meal is a social occasion, requiring attention to the needs of the group in order to make it successful.

Just as being hungry while shopping at the supermarket can lead to uneconomical impulse purchases, listening to one's stomach alone can be the worst way to choose a restaurant. Given the high percentage of available time (and often money) represented by a meal out, it pays to take that few extra minutes to choose the place your group will enjoy most, to drive a few extra minutes or spend a few extra dollars to achieve true enjoyment rather than mere satisfaction of physical needs.

In choosing a restaurant for a group, I don't believe it's always necessary or productive to pander to the lowest common denominator. My wife and I, for example, have divergent dining preferences, and I think we are a fairly typical couple in that regard. If we simply aggregated and averaged our preferences we'd wind up at a lot of "general menu" restaurants eating chicken fingers and fajitas. We prefer to trade off: one night we will choose a place I really love, and her ordering choices and preferences will take a back seat to mine. Another night I will reciprocate. Our sum total of happiness is much higher that way, and sometimes we end up expanding one another's culinary horizons.

After listening to our own preferences and those of our dining companions, we can also hear from a restaurant directly through menus. Before publicists, critics, and other diners refract a restaurant's message through their subjective lenses, most every restaurant has already produced a self-revealing document: the menu. At better restaurants, the menu is a window to the mind of the chef, as it is the chef's only opportunity to communicate directly with the customer, other than through the actual food. Even at a chain restaurant, great care goes into crafting a menu that not only reflects the food, but also the spirit of the place: Do the dishes have silly fun names? Is the menu trying to appeal to a mass market or a core of folks with specific tastes? What are the prices? Is there a structure to the menu, such as a fixed price for several courses (in which case you're going to have a full meal) or a tapas-style array of small plates (in which case you can opt for a quick bite)?

Assuming the kitchen executes its menu with reliable competence, the menu itself is a superb—yet underutilized—tool for predicting whether you will enjoy a restaurant. After all, you know best what you like (a fact overlooked by those who slavishly subvert their preferences to the recommendations of others). These days, most new restaurants and many established ones post their menus on the Web, or menu-oriented Web sites do it for them. Most will also, if you ask, fax you a copy. And nearly every restaurant everywhere posts a menu in the window, so you can check it out before committing to dinner.

Then, once you've dined at a restaurant, take a moment to reflect on what you liked and didn't like. You may find that when planning a dinner you focus mostly on what type of food to eat, as in Italian or Japanese, but you also may find when leaving the restaurant that your enjoyment of your meal was very much dependent on the service you received, or any of a million other factors worth remembering before the cycle begins again. As a writer on assignment, I often don't get to choose where I dine—those choices get made for me by restaurateurs who open new places or hire new chefs, by editors who give me assignments, and by the media's consensus about what restaurants are important. But I always have the power to learn from where I've dined, so that when I dine on my own time and my own dime, I can make better choices.

CHAPTER FIVE

The Business of the
Restaurant Business

Café Gray is counting down the last five weeks before its scheduled opening. I arrive at the third floor of the Time Warner Center, a mighty glass hotel, office, residential, shopping, and dining complex overlooking Central Park and Columbus Circle. I wait until the security guard isn't looking, dart into the Café Gray construction site, and immediately trip over a carton of mirrored black ceiling tiles. Not that there's any ceiling to speak of: there is only a metal grid where the ceiling will eventually go, and I can look up through the ductwork, BX-cables, plumbing, and hanging temporary lights all the way through to the underside of the building's fourth floor, where another restaurant, Per Se, is under heavy reconstruction on account of a fire that broke out during its first week of business.

Café Gray is one of five restaurants opening in the new Time Warner Center in Manhattan, each with one of the world's top chefs at its helm. Thomas Keller, Jean-Georges

Vongerichten, Charlie Trotter, and Masa Takayama join Gray Kunz in what is surely the greatest concentration of culinary talent the world has ever seen under one roof.

It's hard for me to believe there's going to be a dining room here in five weeks, but chef/owner Gray Kunz, his executive chef Larry Finn, and pastry chef Chris Broberg repeatedly assure me that "all the hard work is already done—this is just cosmetic stuff we're working on now." Which may be true if you define floors, walls, and ceilings as "cosmetic stuff."

The purpose of this first visit is to do a walk-through of the under-construction kitchens with the chef, his kitchen team, the construction site manager, and kitchen designer Jimi Yui. In the rarefied world of designers who create multimillion-dollar customized restaurant kitchens, Jimi Yui—whom no normal person has ever heard of—is a superstar. Equal parts designer, contractor, architect, and culinary psychologist, Jimi builds kitchens to the exacting specifications of some of the world's top chefs.

The Café Gray space is a triangle, one side of which is a wall of windows overlooking Central Park and the statue of Christopher Columbus in Columbus Circle—one of the most dramatic views any restaurant could have. Kunz, Yui, and head architect David Rockwell, however, decided to do something totally contrarian: instead of placing the dining room up against the windows and hiding the kitchen in the back, they built a whole-restaurant-length open kitchen right in front of the windows. While counterintuitive, this doubles the drama of the view: customers look past the working kitchen and out onto the park.

"My job," explains Yui, "is to get inside the chef's head and create a kitchen that follows his cooking and organizational style. Over the course of almost a year, I presented Gray with more than twenty different sets of kitchen plans. And this was before we started construction or ordered a single piece of equipment. This kitchen is all about how Gray cooks.

"Even among chefs, Kunz is a major perfectionist," Jimi tells me as we watch Gray Kunz fret over a small pipe that runs up one side of the gargantuan Molteni island stove that forms the kitchen's centerpiece. "This is the kind of stuff that nobody else even notices, but it will drive Gray crazy." The chef doesn't like the chrome finish on the pipe, because it will dull and scratch after repeated cleanings. He wants the pipe to be square, not round, so that it will sit flush against the flat wall of the cooking island. And he wants it to bend in two places, so as to follow the wall exactly.

Over in the dishwashing area, there's a structural support for one of the shelves that Kunz isn't happy with. "You see this?" he says twice. "They're going to bang the dishes into this and it's going to be ten thousand dollars in breakage a year. Can't we support this shelf from the ceiling instead?" Yui and the construction manager exchange a knowing glance—they're not going to talk Kunz out of this. Not that there's a ceiling anyway.

As I snack on some (okay, all) of pastry chef Chris Broberg's lavender-scented white-chocolate-crunch petits fours (at this point the pastry kitchen is the one fully operational part of the restaurant, so there are always plenty of sweets to be had), I read the various schedules, drafts of menus, and to-do lists taped to the wall of the restaurant's temporary office. (Later, this space adjacent to the kitchen will hold a special "chef's table" for private parties.) Today at 3 P.M. there will be CPR training for all the managers. In two weeks, there will be a charity event in the restaurant—they'll erect temporary walls and hide the construction materials during the party, and then go back to construction the next day. The following week the pastry chef has a dentist's appointment. It's all there.

For Gray Kunz, the opening of Café Gray represents a triumph over half a decade of adversity. Standing in the space that was soon to be his first restaurant in so many years, I remember Kunz's departure from Lespinasse in the wake of a bitter labor dispute, and my first lost restaurant love. I remember my last meal, on the last night Kunz was at Lespinasse. I dined alone. My wife, a travel journalist, was on assignment in Alaska and I didn't wish to share the event with anybody else. I ate from 6 P.M. until nearly midnight. It was an epic feast reminiscent of *Big Night*. All my old favorites appeared, yet, even on that last night, new creations continued to emerge from the kitchen. Each member of the waitstaff in turn came by my table to chat. We talked about the future of the restaurant and their plans for the months prior to the arrival of Kunz's replacement. Some of them chose to work at other restaurants for a couple of months—perhaps in the Hamptons (where one very proper French captain told me that he would be placed in the unenviable position of asking people, "How would you like your hamburger cooked?") or perhaps in Manhattan. Others would devote the time to vacation activities—a family reunion in Romania, surfing in Sumatra, or rest and relaxation in Rio. The new chef, Christian Delouvrier, also had vacation plans: he and the general manager were headed off on a European journey of culinary discovery. They planned to visit many of the great restaurants of France, "to see what's going on out there."

At the end of the evening, after all the other guests had departed, I stood alone in the Lespinasse dining room and said goodbye. And then the party started. The party had been casually mentioned to me by Chef Kunz as "a little gathering of a few of my friends to make a toast to the restaurant and maybe have a few hors d'oeuvres." Thus, I was a bit surprised when, at midnight, 150 of Gray Kunz's closest friends showed up, including culinary superstars Daniel Boulud and François Payard—as well as just about every former employee of the Lespinasse kitchen, from the now-famous Rocco DiSpirito to leading New Indian chef Floyd Cardoz. I was further surprised to see that the "hors d'oeuvres" amounted to one of the greatest culinary assemblages I'd ever seen. It was my most perverse food fantasy come to life—all the best dishes in the history of Lespinasse presented as an all-you-can-eat buffet in the kitchen. All the stoves and counters were covered with white tablecloths, and one of the stations became an impromptu bar.

It was clear that this party was to last all night. Many of the guests moved on to a second celebration, hosted by First, a restaurant downtown. I said my farewell to Gray Kunz and thanked him for giving me the greatest culinary memories of my life. "There will be many more, Mr. Shaw, I promise you that," he replied, with tears in his eyes.

It was a long time in coming. Between his resignation from Lespinasse and the launch of Café Gray, Gray Kunz had what seemed like one of the worst runs of bad luck in chefdom, at least for chefs at his level. At first, reports of new Kunz ventures would appear in the press every few months, only to be followed up with stories that the deals had collapsed. Eventually, Kunz faded from the media A-list. In 2003, few people in food writing circles could even say where Gray Kunz was at any given time. It was not until 2004 that the plans for Café Gray really took shape.

The week after my first visit to the construction site, when I was told the restaurant was five weeks from opening, the restaurant is eight weeks from its scheduled opening. This feat of temporal mathematics has not been accomplished through use of a time machine; rather, there have been construction delays.

Gray Kunz and the six core members of his kitchen team are at the stoves. The chef calls out an order: "One risotto, one pork, one soufflé." He then points to the sous-chef at the hot appetizers station and asks: "What do you do?" I slowly realize the stoves aren't on, there are no ingredients at the cooks' stations, and there are no pots or pans. Rather, the kitchen team is going through a theoretical exercise.

"I'll get my risotto rice from this drawer here," says the cook. Kunz nods and makes a check mark on his list. "Then I'll keep the chicken stock . . . over here?" The kitchen team gathers around to inspect the proposed spot.

Kunz doesn't like it. "Someone is going to knock the container over, and it looks shitty to have it in the middle of the stove. This is an open kitchen; we have to keep it neat." In the end, they decide to have the metal fabricator create a special bracket to hold the stock container against one of the stove's structural supports, close enough to the oven's exhaust duct to keep it warm all night.

The hypothetical cooking ballet continues as the pipe-fitters run their electric saw and the demolition team rolls carts of sheetrock scrap around. I notice the ceiling is finally coming together—large parts of it are now closed up. "Okay what was the entree?" asks Kunz. Nobody remembers. It's an awkward moment. Finally I say "pork" and seven heads immediately snap in my direction. Kunz chuckles, and then glares with disapproval at his cooks.

An assistant approaches Kunz with a sample plate, to be used as part of the breakfast service. "Too fancy, too expensive, too formal," judges Kunz. "We're calling ourselves a café. This isn't Lespinasse. People need to be able to eat here every day."

Eight weeks later, Café Gray is eleven weeks from opening. The construction delays have expanded, worsened by the restaurant's dwindling bank accounts. But finally, I get to eat a meal.

There are no tables in the dining room, so Ellen and I sit on two gray metal folding chairs pushed up against a waist-high wall that divides the kitchen from the dining-room-to-be. We drink water from mismatched glasses and eat with assorted silverware from the various sample candidates. The menu is in an early stage of development, so the dishes are experimental. Gray Kunz's experiments, flights of fancy, and mistakes, however, put most chefs' signature dishes to shame. The tastes bring back memories of what I so love about Kunz's food: you take a bite and, after processing its fundamental deliciousness, you say, "What the heck is in this sauce?" And then you take another bite and say, "Hey, is that fennel? And is it pickled?" And each time you take another bite you experience the dish in a whole new way.

Now all the restaurant needs to do is open. The opening date is largely out of Kunz's hands, however, as he depends so much on the resources of the skyscraper he's in, the ability of his backers to pay the bills, and the general atmosphere of chaos surrounding a major opening being pushed through on a rush schedule. There have been so many delays that, at this point, any announced opening date is really just what one publicist I know calls a "hopening."

Meanwhile, in Chicago, Grant Achatz is building a different kind of restaurant from the ground up, literally and figuratively, in a standalone building on a quiet street. His restaurant Alinea—named for an old typographical symbol that indicates the beginning of a new train of thought—is new in every way, from the food to the specially designed dishes it is served on.

All restaurants begin in the mind, but some are more about ideas than others. At Achatz's previous restaurant, Trio, he developed a reputation as one of America's foremost avant-garde chefs. (Before that, he had been at the legendary French Laundry in Napa, as well as in several other top kitchens.) As with the avant-garde in the studio and performing arts, the culinary avant-garde is about questioning assumptions. Most restaurants, for example, maintain basic divisions between savory and sweet foods, serving savories first and concluding with sweets. The avant-garde chef asks, "Why?" and perhaps tries it the other way around. Most restaurants offer menus with entrees consisting of a piece of protein, a starch, and a vegetable. The avant-garde chef asks, "Why?" and perhaps serves no entrees at all, but rather a succession of tastes. These are just a few of the questions the avant-garde chef asks. Achatz, for his part, even questions the use of forks and knives.

In his laboratory, where he will spend the six months prior to Alinea's opening working with his cooking team developing recipes and presentation, Achatz collaborates with designer Martin Kastner of Crucial Detail on several unique serving pieces.

The Achatz-Kastner relationship began when Achatz needed a way to present "frozen suckers"—small spherical ice pops—for dessert. Placing them flat on a plate wouldn't do, so Achatz solicited thirty designers to come up with a serving piece that would hold the suckers upright. Over the course of hundreds of e-mails between Kastner and Achatz, many with three dimensional graphic renderings attached, the two settled not only on an upright sucker-holder with three legs that snap together into a handle when picked up, but on a whole approach to Alinea's serving pieces. "We realized," says Achatz, "that the service of food has remained basically the same for the last two hundred years." Yet, "as food has advanced in technique it has at times become more difficult to serve." Rather than plates, forks, and knives for every dish, then, Alinea would have several serving pieces tailored to its dishes.

A half-dollar-sized frozen disc of sorbet fits into a purpose-made glass holder—Achatz and Kastner call it "the eye"—and is eaten with tongs. Thin crisps and slices of food, instead of being placed flat on a plate, are suspended from a stainless steel device called "the bow." A series of small interlocking mini-trays form "the sectional plate," where each section is picked up and the food is eaten by tilting it into the diner's mouth. A holder for spoons containing individual bites of food is called "the antiplate." Other dishes are concealed in a spherical holder, "the pouch," which the server flips open to reveal the food as the dish is presented. It is a modern-day version of the cloche, or silver dome, that was kept over food in old-style luxury restaurant service.

Every step Achatz's team takes in the laboratory is painstakingly documented. The Alinea team photographs experiments in various states of readiness, the media are invited to observe, and there are constant Web updates. (I've never met Achatz or Kastner in person; they've told me their story via e-mail and in their Weblog, which I helped create, edit, and produce.) This spirit of extroverted documentary rigor is one of the ties that binds many of the leading culinary practitioners. Ferran Adrià, the Spanish avant-garde chef at El Bulli (and one of Achatz's inspirations) has thus far produced three volumes of cookbooks weighing in at approximately ten pounds and five hundred pages each, documenting, year-by-year, every dish that has ever been on his menus. Alain Ducasse has authored or coauthored more than fifteen books, including a three-volume *Grand Livre de Cuisine* series focused on his fine-dining restaurants and a bigger-than-El-Bulli book about his global chain of casual eateries, Spoon. Some might call this ego, and ego is surely a component, but having met with many such chefs I'm sure that it's more about commitment to the craft.

Serving pieces aren't all that must be developed before a restaurant's first plate of food can be served. Achatz and Kastner also work together on a logo for Alinea, attempting to incorporate the sense of aerial motion, newness, and surprise of Achatz's approach to cuisine. And, of course, a business plan must be created as well.

Unless a restaurant is subsidized by a hotel (as many of Alain Ducasse's restaurants are) or by vanity investors willing to take a loss, it will need to make money to survive. Chefs, like many other kinds of entrepreneurs, rarely have enough money to fund any but the smallest mom-and-pop-sized restaurants, and given the high failure rate of restaurants and many chefs' lack of corporate credit and cash-flow history, banks are reluctant to make substantial loans (though some smaller loans are available through the Small Business Administration program). Chefs who want to open restaurants, therefore, need to find investors.

In Achatz's case, he found Nick Kokonas. Like many restaurant investors, Kokonas was a customer first: a successful Chicago-based businessman with a love of haute cuisine, Kokonas had dined all over the world but concluded that his favorite restaurant, Achatz's former stamping ground Trio, was right around the corner. (Kokonas tells the story of a challenge he delivered to two gastronome friends, one from New York and the other from San Francisco: "If the meal at Trio isn't the best meal you've ever had, I'll pay for your meals and your flights." He didn't need to pay.) Kokonas dined at Trio often and developed a friendship with Achatz. But before the culinary relationship could grow into a business relationship, Achatz had to convince Kokonas that he could not only serve great food, but do so profitably.

The single largest expense of most restaurants is rent, so much so that dozens of restaurateurs have told me over the years that "the restaurant business is the real estate business." Real estate issues loom large on the balance sheet and affect operational matters. How many seats will there be, and therefore how many "covers" (individual customers) will the restaurant "do" per day? Where will the restaurant be located, and how will that affect attendance? What kind of construction will need to be done on the kitchen and dining room? What style of space will the restaurant occupy, and how will that affect its message and target market?

"One of the things we felt really strongly about," says Kokonas, "was that we wanted Alinea to be a standalone building, because if you're in something else you can't help but take on some of that identity." Once they agreed on that, and on a general neighborhood in Chicago, Achatz and Kokonas got in the car and drove along every street on the grid, marking maps in red, yellow, and green to indicate levels of enthusiasm for different streets. "After hours of driving, they all seem to blur together," Achatz told me in an e-mail. "Just as a traffic light green was go (good), yellow was maybe and red was no way." They then had a realtor show them every available property on every desirable street that met their requirements.

Real estate may account for the largest single number in a restaurant business plan, but it's not the only one. There are other major expenses, such as payroll, professional fees, and legal work. And there are minor ones. On Kokonas and Achatz's spreadsheets, everything they can imagine is accounted for, right down to "one dustpan @$2.08," and "10 speed pour oil bottles @$2.99 each."

One misconception many people have about restaurants is that they make all their money on the bar. While it's true that an active bar and strong liquor and wine sales can be strong profit centers for restaurants and can help keep the food prices down, most restaurants, of course, would not survive just as bars. The overall profitability of a restaurant can't be reduced to any one factor. It involves sales of food, drink, and often private parties and off-premises catered events. The loss of any one of those income streams can mean the difference between life and death for a restaurant.

Some restaurants, however, do just fine with no or limited alcohol sales. Most fast-food chains in North America sell no alcohol of any kind. In states where licenses are restricted or expensive, such as New Jersey, it is common for fine-dining establishments not to have them and instead to allow BYO. The French Laundry, one of the most profitable restaurants in America with revenues of $7.5 million per year, has no liquor license or bar (it sells wine only) on account of local regulations and its proximity to a school.

There's no way to know when exactly Alinea will open, but given the degree of control Achatz has, it's far more likely that he'll open on time and the way he wants to open than it is that a less autonomous owner like Gray Kunz will.

Though they're very different restaurants, both Alinea and Café Gray are brethren in that they're classic examples of chef-driven restaurants. They represent, each in its own way, the American dream of a chef-restaurateur who is the top person in a restaurant's organization. Not all, or even most, restaurants are chef-driven, however. The restaurant industry is wildly diverse, and there's room for many types of excellence.

Security is tight at 630 Fifth Avenue, one of the mega office buildings in the Rockefeller Center complex. Ever since 9/11, visitors have had to wait in line, check in with security, show a drivers license, and carry a bar-coded visitor's pass that gets scanned upon entry and departure. Every move is tracked. According to my security pass, I arrive at the headquarters of the Starwich Corporation at 9:58 A.M.

Starwich is a projected six weeks away from opening its first sandwich shops—four of them almost at once—in New York City. The business plan calls for quickly following those openings with a dozen additional New York stores, plus branches in Boston, Providence, Washington, D.C., and Philadelphia.

Sitting in their office, surrounded by experimental coffee-cup lids, electronic smart-cards, Starwich baseball caps, and piles of spreadsheets, Spiro Baltas (the CEO) and Michael Ryan (the president) tell me the Starwich story. They had the same kind of thought that so many food lovers have: Why can't we get a decent sandwich anywhere? They wished for a quick, casual, convenient restaurant serving high-quality sandwichy, salady food in a comfortable setting at a reasonable price—like Subway, only better. But instead of just wishing, which is the stage at which I usually bow out of things, they actually did something about it.

By the time you read this book, there may be a Starwich sandwich shop on every major street corner and mall food court in America, right across from the Starbucks. The similarity in names is no coincidence: Starwich hopes to be the Starbucks of sandwiches and salads—if the company has its way, "Starwich will redefine the sandwich shop as Starbucks has redefined the coffee house."

Or, Starwich may fail. Most new restaurants do. But I have a good feeling about these guys, because I like their coffee-cup lids. All good restaurants need to serve good food, but sometimes it's the little non-food items that put them over the top.

The inadequacy of coffee-cup lids has been a pet peeve of mine for years. My wife, Ellen, and I between us must have a dozen pair of ruined trousers from coffee spills in the van—New York City is full of potholes and we put in a lot of time driving around exploring every nook and cranny of the city. The lids with the little oval-shaped holes don't work because the coffee can fly right out through the hole if the van hits a pothole. The lids with the little flaps that peel and lock back don't work for three reasons: I usually destroy the lid when separating the flap, the lock-back mechanism of the flap is prone to fail, and therefore the flap hits me in the nose while I drink, and all this requires so much attention that it's impossible to drive safely while going through the machinations.

Starwich, in conjunction with the Solo cup company, has devised a solution: beneath this new specially designed lid is a rotating plastic disc insert. The lid has a hole, and the disc insert has a hole to match. A little lever-like toggle—almost like a sliding dimmer on a light switch—causes the insert to rotate back and forth. When the holes line up, you can drink. When the holes don't line up, it's like the cylinders of a lock falling into place: the coffee stays in the cup even if you hit a speed bump. It's a totally reliable one-handed operation: the answer to my coffee-cup prayers. It's the sort of innovation that gets a restaurant noticed, and earns repeat business. The coffee also needs to be good.

Bizarrely, I recently had learned that my grandfather Arthur Shaw was a pioneer of insulated coffee cups. But he never, the family history runs, figured out how to make the lids (his problem was that he tried to make the lids out of the same material as the cups). My mother even has his original shares of the now defunct Insul-Cup Corporation. I guess I come by my fixation honestly.

Baltas and Ryan vie for my attention as I spend about an hour playing obsessively with a coffee cup lid while fantasizing about how a successful Insul-Cup Corporation could have given me a life of gentlemanly leisure. "We can give you some of those to take with you," they hint in an attempt to refocus me, "and over here we have our five corporate principles . . ." I'm not sure what those principles are, because when I left the corporate world I swore I'd never read another business plan, but the general idea is that Starwich is all about the details: making sandwiches and salads isn't rocket science, but it needs to be done just so.

Starwich's plan is to issue each customer a "smart card," a small plastic credit card–sized device with an embedded computer chip. The Starwich smart card remembers your name, your three favorite sandwich combinations (right down to special requests like "extra mayo"), and your last ten orders. Customers can also access their profiles online, where they can add money to a virtual account that lets them pay for sandwiches with the smart card (if you add $50, you get $55 worth of credit).

Both gentlemen, now in their mid-thirties, are veteran restaurant employees and managers. They met when they both worked at BR Guest, Inc., one of New York's largest and most successful restaurant groups—if you have ever been to New York City and dined at Blue Water Grill or Ruby Foo's, you've been to a BR Guest restaurant. Over time, each revealed to the other a longstanding ambition to open a high-quality sandwich shop. Starwich is the result of the combination of their visions.

Just about the last thing a middle class parent wants to hear is that the eldest son has decided to work in a restaurant or hotel—and not as the chef or owner. It's almost as bad as learning that he's going to become a janitor or, worse, a food writer. "I was the black sheep in my family," says Baltas. "No one in my family considered running restaurants a 'real' job."

Yet many restaurants are multimillion-dollar businesses, as complex and "legitimate" as (and now it turns out as likely to stay in business as) the most cutting-edge computer companies. Baltas's family came around after watching him orchestrate the operations of several large restaurants and restaurant groups. "It was an eye-opener," he says with obvious triumph, "for my family to see that the restaurant industry is very much big business."

Baltas's first job out of college had him working as the morning front desk manager at a Marriott hotel near his home town of Boston. But, like me, he can't stand getting up early in the morning. So he jumped on an opportunity to move into a management position at the hotel's restaurant—at night. He was hooked.

Like many outsiders coming into The Life, Baltas was particularly surprised by the amount of technology and advanced business modeling behind a major restaurant operation. He threw himself into learning the computer systems and models and later parlayed his expertise into a position at La Familia, an Italian family-style restaurant mini-empire with two restaurants doing a combined $5 million a year in the Boston area. "They may have gotten more than they bargained for. I catapulted them into the twentieth century by installing computers, establishing service standards, and introducing promotions. They believed in me and encouraged me, but at first I know they were thinking, 'who is this guy?'" Two years later, Baltas had transformed La Familia into a five-restaurant group generating $20 million in sales annually. He quickly became a sought-after restaurant industry consultant.

After a stint at the Four Seasons Hotel in Boston, where he learned the wine side of the business, Baltas came to New York in 1998 as restaurant and wine director of the legendary Tavern on the Green restaurant. Later, he worked for the Sbarro restaurant group (which, in addition to the shopping-mall Italian eateries it operates worldwide, also runs fine-dining restaurants in New York) and the BR Guest group. That's where he met Michael Ryan.

At age sixteen, Ryan took his first job baking pizzas at a local pizzeria in Glen Ellyn, Illinois. He made pizzas there for seven years, paying his way through college in pursuit of a degree in advertising. In college, in addition to his pizza duties, he managed a fraternity-house kitchen and did stints around town as a waiter, cook, and assistant restaurant manager. He became a restaurant-business junkie—he never did pursue that career in advertising. Instead, he joined a small team of entrepreneurs to start up a fine-dining dinner cruise ship company called Odyssey Cruises in Chicago. This eight-hundred-passenger vessel had, in its first year, sales of over $13 million. In 1997, Ryan became regional operations director at Lettuce Entertain You Enterprises. Founded by industry legend Rich Melman, this company built restaurants such as Shaw's Crab House, Mity Nice Grill, and Vong Chicago, which together generate more than $25 million annually. Three years later, Ryan moved to New York City to become director of operations for BR Guest, with restaurants that collectively gross more than $100 million a year.

So why, with all this background at the high end of the industry, would Baltas and Ryan want to open a chain of sandwich shops? For one thing, sandwiches are currently a $150 billion business—one of the largest segments of the restaurant industry. There's a lot more money in sandwiches than in fancy French restaurants. For another thing, both Baltas and Ryan felt something was missing—an empty niche existed in the restaurant business: a quick-casual, high-quality sandwich operation. And for still another thing, they themselves wanted a place to eat. "I was annoyed," says Baltas, "that every time I wanted to take my wife and kids out for a quick bite I had to either overpay at a fancy restaurant or eat crap at a chain."

But more important, I think, is an emerging trend: many of the best people in the business are focusing on the middle and lower ends of the market. For example, chef Tom Colicchio operates three highly successful upscale restaurants: Gramercy Tavern and Craft in Manhattan and Craftsteak in Las Vegas. Yet his most recent restaurant ventures have been sandwich shops called 'wichcraft (with locations in Manhattan and Las Vegas, and more planned). Alain Ducasse, arguably the world's preeminent French chef, has lately focused his attention on a chain of casual eateries called Spoon. Gray Kunz and Jean-Georges Vongerichten, two of America's top haute cuisine chefs, have collaborated on the Spice Market, a restaurant specializing in the street foods of Southeast Asia. As the American consumer becomes more savvy about food, the demand for better food at every level rises, and the sheer volume and cost effectiveness of casual dining—no maitre d', no fine crystal, no lovebirds taking up a table for three hours—make it the logical new market for the best chefs and restaurateurs. After all, good food is good food. Excellence doesn't have to come in a fancy package.

This isn't the sort of business one starts with money borrowed from mom and dad. Starwich is a serious venture capital operation. In order to raise money, Baltas and Ryan needed to assemble a compelling proposal and shop it around to hundreds of venture capitalists. That they decided to undertake this effort in the middle of a full-blown recession, knowing full well that restaurant investments are considered some of the riskiest long shots in the venture capital universe, is a testament either to bravery, idealism, or insanity.

But eventually Baltas—who took the lead on making sales pitches to potential investors—got Starwich its first $50,000 check from an investor, and from there it was a steady crawl to the $2 million needed to open the first six Starwich stores. During that time, Baltas made ten or more pitches per week for nearly a year. Often during the early pitches, the larger, more experienced investors would ask Baltas questions to which he had no answers. "I didn't even speak the language. But we locked ourselves in our office until we had the answers. Eventually, we had them all. We hope!"

In the end, though, Starwich's success will depend on the answer to the question "Where should we go for dinner?" Or, in this case, lunch. For the business to work, a sufficient number of people will have to answer "Starwich" to that question. Starwich hopes that everybody will love its sandwiches, but it is specifically targeted at two groups: the "corporate consumer" and "young, newly settled couples."

Still, Starwich will have to sell a lot of $9 sandwiches and salads to pay the rent, cover its employees' salaries, and earn back several million dollars for its investors. "Sure, we're taking a risk," Baltas says. "But what's the worst thing that can happen? We go back to our old jobs?"

Finally, the first Starwich store opens. On my first visit I tuck into the Soft-Shell Crab BLT and breathe a sigh of relief: it's excellent, and the store is as comfortable and hospitable as the Starwich partners said it would be. I think Starwich is going to make it.

In Wilson, North Carolina, Ed Mitchell is presiding over his new "pig bar," one of several barbecue concepts he hopes to franchise in the coming years. The pig bar looks like any bar, anywhere, right down to the beer taps, dark wood, and television screens playing sports programming, but where you'd normally find liquor bottles on the back bar there is, instead, a bathtub-sized multicompartment apparatus holding different cuts of pit-roasted pork. Customers at the pig bar point to what they want, and the pig-bartender makes up a plate. "People eat with their eyes," comments Mitchell. "And this will get them hungry."

I met Ed Mitchell in New York City at a block party. He and his crew, including his brothers Aubrey and Stevie and his son Ryan, had driven up to Manhattan from Wilson in a semi truck filled with barbecue equipment in order to participate in the Big Apple Barbecue Block Party. There were several other participants in the event—pitmasters had come from as far away as Texas—but two things immediately struck me about Ed Mitchell: first, he was the only African-American pitmaster at the event. All the others were white, as are most barbecue restaurant owners in the South despite the genre's largely black roots. Second, he was the only one barbecuing whole hogs. The rest were cooking ribs, pork shoulder, and other small-by-comparison cuts of meat.

At a panel discussion on the meaning of barbecue, Mitchell sat quietly on the dais with the other pitmasters. The others had plenty to say but, like a professional poker player, Mitchell just watched. A bear of a man, he cut quite a figure in his overalls, baseball cap, and massive white beard. When the rest of the crew was all talked out, Mitchell finally leaned forward toward his microphone and said, "May I add just a couple of comments?" At which point the crowd was treated to a quiet, intensive lecture on the social history of barbecue. Mitchell, among other surprises, has a masters degree in sociology. I knew then that, one day, I'd have to visit Mitchell on his home turf.

Mitchell's Ribs Chicken & BBQ, home to the pig bar, rises out of Wilson, North Carolina's spartan landscape, like a secret government research hangar. With few surrounding reference points, the scale of the operation isn't entirely clear until you're standing right in front of it: Mitchell's barn-like structure is large enough to accommodate a large herd of cattle or a small shopping mall. By 11 A.M. the parking lot is filling with cars and tour buses—what are people doing on tours around here anyway?—and over in a far corner of the lot's expanse is the same semi truck I had seen in New York City the previous summer.

It didn't start out this way. Although as a boy he had assisted his father at many a pig roast—he recalls every occasion being transformed into an excuse for a pig roast, from birthdays to the birth of a favorite hunting dog's litter—Ed Mitchell never intended to run a barbecue restaurant. His G.I. bill–funded studies ranged from sociology to economics, and he spent seventeen years as a manager for Ford in Boston. It wasn't until his father took ill, and he came back home to help care for his family, that the barbecue idea was hatched.

The current Mitchell's site used to be the Mitchell family grocery. Like most small stores of its kind, Mitchell's grocery eventually came under pressure from chain supermarkets and evolving tastes. With Mitchell's father unable to work the store, the pressure on his mother was almost unbearable. One day, as Ed Mitchell was helping his mother open the store, she began to cry on account of the mounting pressure of a dying husband and a struggling business.

"What can I do to make you feel better?" he asked.

"Make me some of your barbecue," she answered, "like you used to make."

So Mitchell, a dutiful son, went out and bought a baby pig and spent the day barbecuing it. Near closing time, it was ready.

Mitchell recalls eating the barbecue behind the counter with his mother, when a customer walked in. "Oh, Mrs. Mitchell, you've got barbecue now?" The rest was history.

Ed Mitchell sees his restaurant—now more than ten times the size of the family market—as a research laboratory. Rooted in the Southern barbecue tradition, Mitchell is nonetheless a modernist, and his goal is to unite the old methods with contemporary business acumen to create a barbecue empire that can expand and replicate itself beyond Wilson, and beyond Mitchell's lifetime. "I'm doing this for my son," he said several times during the day I spent with him.

And so, unlike most Southern barbecue establishments, Mitchell's is decidedly high-tech. At the drive-through window, the employees wear wireless headsets and utilize the same computer point-of-sale ordering systems as Kentucky Fried Chicken. At the main service line, Mitchell has inverted the traditional barbecue kitchen by putting all the food out in the open: customers line up cafeteria-style and point to whatever they want, and the staff builds each person a plate. "People eat with their eyes," was another of Mitchell's oft-repeated comments. The cafeteria line also allows Mitchell to service easily in excess of a thousand customers a day. "We've never even tested the limits of this thing." Yet despite the streamlined look and feel of Mitchell's, everything in the back of the house occurs with old-fashioned rigor. Hushpuppies are shaped by hand (most barbecue places, even the most traditional ones, now use a machine), desserts are made from scratch, and vegetables are prepared according to old Mitchell family recipes.

"I'm developing different styles for different audiences, so there'll be something for everyone," Mitchell says of his franchise plans. "You want a quick bite, there's the drive-through, just like at the KFC. You want a quick meal here, you go through the service line. In the back we'll have table service. And at the pig bar, you can get together with your buddies, have some beer and some pig, and watch the game."

Perhaps most innovative, however, is Mitchell's system for pit-roasting whole hogs, a system he calls "banking." North Carolina barbecue, in the eastern part of the state where Mitchell is from, is synonymous with the whole hog. While it's a fairly simple matter to create automated equipment for roasting chickens or racks of ribs, nobody before Mitchell has attempted to create a scientifically based system for pit-roasting whole hogs. Thus, whole-hog barbecue remains the most mysterious form of barbecue, requiring 24/7 attention and continuous adjustment to the barbecue pits, and is practiced only by a few idiosyncratic pitmasters at hard-to-reach locations in the rural South.

What Mitchell's system achieves is a degree of standardization that can allow a properly trained employee to pit-roast a pig like the great pitmasters, without the need to stay up all night. Mitchell's specially constructed all-brick above-ground "pits" are wired with temperature probes, they have special valves to control airflow, and they are backed up by redundant state-of-the art exhaust and fire-suppression systems. For each weight of hog, Mitchell's team has computer-generated graphs demonstrating the pit temperature and internal temperatures for the entire length of the roast. So it is possible, using his system, for the cook to prep and leave the pig on the fire at night, reduce the pit's airflow to the proper level for that size animal, and return in the morning to a fully barbecued whole hog. Then, in the morning, the quicker-cooking items like ribs and chicken can be added to the pits, and by lunchtime there's a full barbecue inventory ready to serve.

When I enter the room housing Mitchell's pits—they are indoors at the back of the restaurant, right where any standard restaurant kitchen would be—I'm reminded of my first barbecue road trip through North Carolina, Tennessee, and Texas. As I set out on the trip, I vowed to visit the pits everywhere I could. I figured there would be resistance—pitmasters have a reputation for secretiveness—but I'd persevere and get behind the scenes. At Wilbur's barbecue in Goldsboro, North Carolina, I summoned up the courage to ask, "May we see the pits?"

"You want to see the pits?" asked a puzzled owner, chewing a cigar and leaning against his white pickup truck. "Sure." We walked around back to a long brick shed lined with smokestacks exhaling gray soot and vaporized grease, and Wilbur opened the door and gestured for us to enter.

It was like walking into an oven, in Hell, without any air, surrounded by the sight, aroma, and vapor of dead baby pigs. I lasted just long enough to have the vision recur to me over the years in early morning nightmares. I didn't ask for very many pit tours after that. Wilbur was, I think, amused.

In Mitchell's pits, the thermometer on the wall reads 70 degrees. There is no aroma. The pigs are under metal domes and, in moments of denial, even look kind of cute. You can read a book, take a nap, or have a picnic in Mitchell's pit area and never know there are whole hogs roasting six feet away from you. And by extension, you may be able to have a Mitchell's barbecue franchise next door to your apartment in a large city yet not be inconvenienced. That, at least, is Ed Mitchell's hope.

"Once this place is set up and the franchises are flying solo, I'm going to get in that barbecue truck and drive. We'll go to festivals, we'll make barbecue everywhere. That's my retirement."

A year later, Ed Mitchell is back with his crew at the second annual Big Apple Barbecue Block Party. This time he's expecting an even larger crowd than last year's, and he's preparing ten whole hogs of approximately 150 pounds each. Now an Ed Mitchell groupie, I hang around with his crew for most of the weekend. On the last day, as a particularly fearsome hog comes off the smoker, Mitchell holds up a pair of thick black welder's gloves and signals to me, "You ready to pick a whole hog?"

Even through those gloves, the steaming flesh of the hog sends burning sensations through my hands and up my arms. By the time I pull the meat out of half the hog and place it in a plastic bin, I'm drenched with perspiration. By the time I finish the hog, I'm about to pass out. Not satisfied to have me still conscious, Ed Mitchell holds up two cleavers: "You ready to chop the hog?"

I make it through about five pounds of meat before my forearms go numb and I slink off to sit on a nearby park bench, eating one of Mitchell's chopped barbecue sandwiches while nursing my wounded hands, arms, and pride.

Café Gray, Alinea, Starwich, and Mitchell's are, I hope, all ventures headed for success and expansion. The tie that binds, however, is that they are all businesses in early stages of entrepreneurial development. Growth is one thing, but how do already-established restaurant businesses hold on to what they already have? How do they keep their edge?

Few people outside the restaurant industry have ever heard of Richard Coraine. Yet he is one of the most important people in the business. Coraine directs the operations of the Union Square Hospitality Group (USHG), which owns five (and counting) prestigious New York restaurants. In the Zagat Survey's 50 most popular New York restaurants, the number 1 and number 2 positions belong to USHG's Union Square Café, and Gramercy Tavern. Two other USHG properties are in the top 20: Tabla and Eleven Madison Park. It probably won't be long before the group's latest venture, Blue Smoke (a high-concept barbecue joint and jazz club) breaks into the elite group as well, at which point 10 percent of New York's fifty most popular restaurants will be operated by a single company.

Not that you could tell that the individual restaurants are part of an empire. Each is an independent operation, looking to the USHG entity for support and management. As a result, five very different restaurants have excellent service, enjoyable surroundings, and a much higher degree of culinary consistency than is the unfortunately low norm.

If you are a reader of newspaper food sections, you may have heard of Coraine's business partner, Danny Meyer—a restaurant industry icon and the father of enlightened American hospitality. Meyer is the public figure, the spiritual leader, and the voice of the USHG. Coraine operates quietly, behind the scenes, to make everything work.

In a business where most ventures don't survive their first year, how can one company so consistently succeed? Moreover, what is the business behind the restaurant business? And what is the restaurant industry's place in the larger context that makes up a community? In an attempt to answer these questions, I shadowed Richard Coraine (everybody calls him 'RC') through the labyrinth of behind-the-scenes USHG goings-on, and I had to set my alarm early to do it.

At 6:30 A.M. on any given day, you'll find RC in his office halfway through a pile of newspapers, surrounded by desk artifacts ranging from bottles of wine and sample takeout drink cups to a fax machine and an iPod. He's not only reading the food, lifestyle, and entertainment sections from newspapers across the country, but is also zeroing in on the business sections. He's learning about his customers, many of whom will be in the newspaper on a given day and most of whom work for companies that are frequent players in those pages.

We begin with an inspection of Eleven Madison Park. RC believes that, standing just inside a restaurant's front door, an experienced observer can tell everything about how the restaurant will perform. "My job is to read the restaurant, and make editorial changes before problems arise."

At 7 A.M., the restaurant is already active, even though there will be no customers until nearly noon. The USHG's assistant florist, Z, is inspecting the floral arrangements and talking on his cell phone to the head florist, Roberta Bendavid, about which stems will need to be replaced. They speak with the seriousness of corporate lawyers planning a leveraged buyout.

RC walks to the podium and activates the reservations computer, quickly scrolling through the names of every customer with reservations today. Any names he recognizes, he pulls up customer notes and often adds to them. At one point he asks me the name of the friend I had dined with at another USHG restaurant a few weeks ago. "Ken Matthews," I tell him. He pulls up my friend Ken's record and adds a notation: "Dines with Steven Shaw," linking to my customer notes.

Today, Eleven Madison Park seems ship-shape to me, but RC is uneasy. "I don't like what I'm seeing today," he says. When I try to get him to clarify, he points to seemingly picayune issues such as the bearing of the managers and the speed with which the employees are walking around the room. "We're going to need to check in here again before lunch," he warns.

On the way out, RC notices a smudge on the wall peeking out from behind a chair stored in a hallway. He pulls every chair away from the wall to reveal a longer smudge where the chair-backs press against the wall. Summoning one of the maintenance staff, he asks that this part of the wall be repainted that morning. "The color codes are on file at the Janovic paint shop around the corner," he adds.

As we walk toward Union Square Cafe, RC goes over his to-do list. A valued employee is getting married that coming weekend and USHG is providing the facilities. In addition, the USHG is building a "Shake Shack" in Madison Square Park, where during the summer they'll sell gourmet frankfurters, hamburgers, and frozen custard. The shack will be staffed mostly by interns from the Culinary Institute of America and various restaurant and hotel management schools. "A hot dog cart or a food kiosk is a very pure expression of the restaurant business," RC explains, himself both an MBA and a culinary school graduate. "It's a great place to learn the fundamentals that hold true no matter how high you go in the industry." On top of that, USHG is in the process of constructing a fine-dining restaurant, a café, and a food kiosk in the Museum of Modern Art, to be timed with the museum's reopening after a long renovation. And in two weeks USHG will be hosting the Big Apple Barbecue Block Party, bringing together America's top pitmasters with great jazz musicians and thousands of hungry, curious New Yorkers.

At Union Square Cafe, Christopher Russell, the restaurant's beverage and service director, is in the wine cellar with sales representative Yoav Sisley, tasting wines from the Admiral Wine Merchants portfolio.

The amount of effort Russell puts into building the Union Square Cafe wine list, maintaining the inventory, and training the staff is staggering. Every day, for what most people would consider two shifts, he's tasting, meeting, teaching, counting, and typing. As I watch him go through the process of creating purchase orders and tasting notes just to add one new wine to the restaurant's list (getting onto the Union Square Cafe wine list is tantamount to getting into Harvard or Yale; of all the wines the sales rep showed Russell today, he purchased only one), I think about the often-heard objection to restaurant wine prices.

I'll be the first to agree that most restaurants charge too much for uninspired wine selections, serve them at improper temperatures in poor stemware, and do not have staff members who adequately understand wines and their relationship to food. At the same time, I fear there is a degree of reductionism in the argument "why should I pay double (or triple, or quadruple) for the same bottle of wine in a restaurant that I could buy in a wine store and drink at home?" I think that the bottle itself creates a conceptual fiction, that because the wine is sealed in that bottle the restaurant cannot add value to it the way the kitchen can add value to a piece of meat. Interestingly, this objection is rarely heard with respect to cocktails, which on a cost basis are more heavily marked up.

But wine is transformed in other ways, some of them contextual and nearly intangible. For one thing, there is a cost involved in being able to choose the right wine for what you decide to order at any given moment. For another thing, there are all the costs of storage, glassware, insurance, and the like. But most importantly, at a great restaurant there is the cost of knowledge.

At Union Square Cafe, for example, there is a staff wine tasting every single day. At family meal, Russell or one of his assistant managers pours tastes from a bottle from the restaurant's wine list. And these are not just the $30 bottles. Every single wine on the list goes through the tasting rotation, so that eventually the servers have all tried, discussed, and compared every wine—even the ones that cost $300 or more.

Later, RC, Christopher Russell, and the restaurant's general manager, Randy Garutti, hold their weekly steering-committee meeting. On tap for today: several upcoming announcements that are likely to anger the waitstaff. A new accounting system will delay receipt of tips and possibly divert more money to the IRS, but the restaurant feels it is the fiscally and legally responsible move. In addition, the restaurant plans to increase the size of its waitstaff, which can potentially mean less in tips for each individual waiter. Although, the hope is that the restaurant will be able to serve more customers and sell them more add-ons, like dessert wine, thus ultimately increasing tips. They settle on their pitch to the waitstaff, though nobody is really looking forward to that particular staff meeting. Throughout the meeting, RC polishes some of the restaurant's glass shelves.

RC spends all of five minutes at Gramercy Tavern,

which I have found to be the most reliable of the group's restaurants. It is here that I first begin to understand the phenomenon of being able to size up an entire restaurant from the front door. Gramercy Tavern, as soon as we enter, gives off a bright, confident feeling of everything being in its place. After chatting with the manager on duty for just a minute and scrolling through the reservations (which he does at every restaurant), he says, "Let's get out of here. All I can do is distract them. They're on the ball and don't need my interference."

At Blue Smoke, the USHG's barbecue restaurant, we enter through the service entrance and almost step on a pig. "This entrance is a mess; we need to get somebody focused on it." A holiday weekend is coming up, and several managers are on vacation. But after meeting with the assistant managers who will be running the restaurant for the weekend, RC is satisfied that, with a little direction, they'll run a tight ship.

Before we enter Tabla, the USHG's contemporary Indian fusion restaurant, RC notices an eight-foot piece of plywood leaning up against the entrance. "Not a good sign," he says to me. Just inside the door, there are four cases of beer that have been delivered and seemingly just abandoned near the podium. RC goes upstairs to find the chef, Floyd Cardoz, who it turns out is busy giving an interview to a reporter from *Gourmet* magazine. "Okay, that explains it," says RC. He grabs a manager and they quickly make a list of what needs to get fixed up around the restaurant. On the way out, RC grabs half an egg sandwich from the staff meal table and eats it as we walk the half-block back to Eleven Madison Park.

As RC had predicted, the scene at Eleven Madison Park

fifteen minutes prior to opening is a bit chaotic. There is no music coming out over the sound system, and he goes to remedy that. He selectively raises his voice with a few of the managers in order to motivate them to crisp up their performance (each time he does so, he winks at me to indicate that it's all really an act). As the first customers arrive, RC retreats into his office and begins an afternoon of transactions and meetings.

By the time the dinner rush gets going, RC is home. "Once they start serving food, my job is done. It has to be done: smooth service is all about preparation and getting up that critical level of momentum. Once it starts, if they still need me, they're doomed."

As we have seen, the director of a successful restaurant spends substantial time every day dealing with issues of staffing, particularly the service staff. But on account of the system by which waitstaff are compensated—tips from customers—there's only so much RC can do to keep them satisfied. The ability of a restaurant to flourish and survive is strongly affected by the quality of waitstaff the restaurant can attract, which in turn is determined largely by how much tip income the servers can make, yet the tipping decision is left solely to the customer.

This sounds like a good deal for us, the customers. But is it really a good system, and does it work the way we think it should?

Certainly, if you are a bad tipper, you'll be fighting an uphill battle to get good service. And if you routinely pass around hundred-dollar bills, you will probably be treated very well. But for the rest of us, for whom tips normally fall into the 15 to 20 percent range, do they really influence the service we get? And why, in the world's most generous nation of tippers, where consumers think nothing of plunking down an additional 15 to 20 percent on top of the bill and sales tax, is service not uniformly excellent? Something has gone wrong, and I think it is the tipping system itself.

In making the case against the tipping system, I emphatically am not endorsing any sort of civil disobedience: as long as the current system is in place, I believe as a good restaurant customer one has a moral obligation to participate in it. A tip, after all, is not really a "gratuity." It is the server's salary: in most states, servers don't even get paid minimum wage by their employers—there is an exemption (called a "credit") for tipped employees that allows restaurants to pay them just a token couple of dollars an hour (as of this date, as low as $1.59 per hour in Kansas and $3.50 per hour in New York City).

And I'm under no illusions that the tipping system will be ended any time soon. There are, after all, three constituencies, comprising the entire relevant population, all of whom are overwhelmingly committed to that system: consumers (who believe it is their God-given right to control the tip), servers (who believe it is their God-given right to receive the tip), and restaurant owners (who believe it is their God-given right to have consumers pay servers, so they don't have to pay their employees a living wage).

It's worth asking, though, whether the tipping system actually serves any of those constituencies, especially in the long term.

Consumers tend to justify the practice of tipping as an incentive: "Waiters know that they won't get paid if they don't do a good job," is the way most advocates of the tipping system (meaning most everybody in America) would put it. To be sure, this is a seductively rational statement about economic theory, but it appears to have little applicability to the real world of restaurants.

For one thing, the American public tends not to apply tips in an economically rational manner. In every survey I've seen, American diners have admitted en masse to tipping a flat amount no matter what and rarely departing upward or downward except in the most extraordinary circumstances. Waiters have, likewise, overwhelmingly testified that good service barely increases the chances of getting a better tip, and that mediocre service barely reduces those chances. I can assure you, based on my own observations, that this is the case. And of course, because so many customers are weak willed, aggressive hustling for tips is often rewarded while low-key, quality service often goes unrecognized.

In addition, the practice of tip pooling, which is the norm in almost every restaurant in America above the level of a greasy spoon, has gutted whatever effect the procedure of voting with your tip might have had on an individual waiter. In a perverse, Maoist outcome, you are actually punishing the good waiters in the restaurant by not tipping the bad one.

Finally, it is a sad reality that American customers often behave unethically with regard to tipping. Many are simply cheap—they take advantage because they know there is no enforcement mechanism requiring them to tip well for good service. Others are clueless and don't understand, for example, that a cooking error has nothing to do with the waiter and that the cooks are not part of the tip pool (as you might imagine, some vindictive cooks have been known to intentionally mishandle the orders of the waiters they dislike, because they know a waiter is far more likely to be punished for unsatisfactory food than for any other reason). Still more are simply evil and this is the one unchecked expression of raw power they have in their pathetic little lives. And don't get me started on the international tourists and their tipping practices.

For another thing, as an empirical matter, there appears to be little causal relationship between the existence of tipping and good service. The best service in the Western world is at the Michelin three-star restaurants of Europe, where there is no tipping. This is because the waiters at the best restaurants of Europe are professionals, trained in professional service academies and driven by the same desire for excellence that makes any professional do a job well despite the absence of tipping. Most top restaurants in America, where there is tipping, come in a distant second when compared to their Michelin-starred rivals. The rest of the restaurants in Europe and America are a mixed bag—I've experienced extremes of service at restaurants in every country I've visited. The only country where I've never had bad service is Singapore. Despite an aggressive market economy, though, there is no tipping in Singapore. British service tends toward the abominable, to be sure, but I think the primary explanation for that is a limited gastronomic tradition in that country. In most of Canada, where there is tipping, service is almost as bad as in the United Kingdom.

As a customer, it's certainly pleasant to dine in France where the menu prices typically represent actual totals, including the price of food, all taxes, and service. I also recall with great fondness a vacation at a "super-inclusive" resort in Jamaica. I certainly found the service to be first rate and, moreover, I found it incredibly relaxing not to be constantly on the alert about tipping everybody.

Waitstaff, for their part, believe they will make more money under the tipping system than they will as salaried employees. And that's probably true. The tipping system, after all, makes waiters into independent contractors. And in any business the hourly wage of a contractor is higher than that of an employee. Yet in most businesses, people choose to be employees.

That is because those who wish to guarantee their long-term financial security have always sacrificed a little bit of quick cash for longer-term benefits like medical insurance, retirement plans, and vacation pay. But, of course, most waitstaff see themselves as transient employees—waiting tables before moving on to bigger and better things. (I might suggest that the large number of waiters I see in their forties, fifties, and sixties puts the lie to this theory.) Moreover, the lack of job security in the business of waiting tables creates a cycle whereby transient employees are the ones primarily attracted to the business in the first place. Contrast that with the back of the house, where kitchen employees receive no tips and typically earn less money than waitstaff, despite the fact that those employees may be graduates of culinary school and have a lifelong commitment to the craft. They focus on the future: rising in rank, and perhaps someday opening a place of their own. They accept a bit less in the here and now in exchange for what they hope will be their part of the American dream.

I've found in my discussions with waiters that it's only the most skilled, experienced waiters—the ones who truly are professionals—who tend to favor the service charge instead of tipping, and this is primarily because they place a higher value on their professionalism and dignity than on the one or two percentage points of income they'd lose in the switch.

Restaurateurs know the tipping system makes their bookkeeping easier. They prefer the current system because it allows them to have a team of independent contractors rather than employees, and these days a top priority of any business is, understandably, to have as few employees as possible (the predictable response to unreasonable labor and tax laws). But that too is shortsighted. Over time, waiters loyal to the company will perform better, sell more, and make customers happier than waiters loyal only to themselves.

People often ask me what restaurant has the best service in America. I always answer: McDonald's. I'm only half joking. While the service at McDonald's lacks finesse, I find that the service at the average McDonald's is far more reliable and consistent than the service at the average upper-middle-market sit-down restaurant. This is not because the employees of McDonald's are so brilliant at their jobs but, rather, because they are well trained and subject to rigorous supervision, all within a system that has been engineered to be as foolproof and consistent as possible. At McDonald's, of course, there is no tipping.

CHAPTER SIX

The Future of Dining

When I ran a search on Google for Jean-Jacques Rachou, I didn't find a single biography or news article about him. Instead, I found only mentions of Rachou in other people's bios, a laundry list of now-famous chefs—Todd English, Charlie Palmer, Gray Kunz, Rick Moonen, Waldy Malouf, Kerry Simon—all of whom trained under Rachou.

Another name many in my generation have never heard is Georges Briguet of the restaurant Le Perigord. Yet the names of those who worked under Briguet are some of the most prominent in the recent history of American cuisine: David Bouley, Thomas Keller, and Antoine Bouterin.

My examination of restaurants and restaurant culture in this book has been very personal and, by virtue of my age, contemporary (I was born in 1969). But I felt my work wouldn't be complete without historical context: this book is a snapshot of the present, but what of the past? And without an understanding of the past, how is it possible to discuss the future?

One of the earliest fine dining experiences I had in New

York was at Rachou's famous La Côte Basque. By the time I started dining out at haute cuisine establishments in earnest, in the early 1990s, La Côte Basque had long been a piece of history. It looked exactly as one would have imagined a fancy New York French restaurant would look in an early Hollywood color film, with its red leather banquettes, tuxedoed waiters, and wraparound mural of a French Mediterranean coastal village. I was swept away by the experience, and I had the finest cassoulet of my life, yet I couldn't help but notice something: I was by far the youngest person in the restaurant.

I continued to frequent La Côte Basque over the years, and it was one of the special occasion restaurants to which I'd take my wife for lunch. Over time, though, as new flavors and an improved American culinary culture descended upon New York, I forgot about La Côte Basque. So did many others. It was, I suppose, only a matter of time, given the restaurant's aging clientele and declining relevance among younger customers, before La Côte Basque would become an economically unsustainable venture.

As I began to work on this book, the word came down from Jean-Jacques Rachou, the chef-owner: La Côte Basque, which had operated continuously since 1958 (and had been owned by Rachou since 1979) was to close its doors forever in early 2004.

This news was almost immediately followed by the announcement that Lutèce, another of the city's grand old French restaurants, was to close, leaving the number of traditional French fine-dining restaurants in New York City at just three: La Grenouille, La Caravelle, and Le Perigord. And in May of 2004, La Caravelle threw in the towel as well.

Such a turn of events would have been unimaginable to a New York restaurant consumer in the 1960s or 1970s. Bob Lape, the long-time restaurant critic for CBS radio and *Crain's New York Business* magazine, recalls "dozens" of formal French restaurants dotting the city during that era, and the former *New York Times* critic Bryan Miller reports that his research through old restaurant guidebooks and articles reveals at least twenty-five such restaurants operating in New York in 1975.

The most traditional of the surviving French stalwarts is Le Perigord. Georges Briguet, an old friend of Rachou's and also one of New York's most venerable restaurateurs, has operated the restaurant since 1964. As the others were closing, Le Perigord was celebrating its fortieth anniversary, making it the longest-running continuously owned (by a single owner) and operated restaurant in New York City.

I cavalierly approached more than a hundred of the top people in the American restaurant business—most of them strangers to me—for interviews, tours, and behind-the-scenes access in the course of writing this book, and virtually all said yes. But when it came to Rachou and Briguet, two giants of New York restaurant history, I confess I was intimidated. Given all they have seen, and all those they have trained, would they even speak to, care about, or acknowledge a writer of my generation? Amazingly, they not only agreed to sit down with me for a discussion of the past, present, and future of American fine dining, but they fought over which of their restaurants would host the dinner.

Given that La Côte Basque was just a few days from closing, though, Rachou prevailed. And, for the last time, I got to eat the cassoulet.

Because he has watched so much of New York's restaurant history unfold, I also invited Bob Lape. Since 1970 he has reviewed more than nine thousand restaurants. (By comparison, in the few years I actively reviewed restaurants, I covered about five hundred. To me that felt like a lot.) And because she is an aficionado of historical restaurant properties and one of my most trusted dining companions, I also asked Shelley Clark, the longtime publicist for, among others, the Waldorf=Astoria Hotel, to join our roundtable.

Clark, Lape, and I are standing at the La Côte Basque bar—Lape and I are plotting our cassoulet order—when Briguet walks in (Rachou is still in the kitchen, where he spends most days and nights, handling the dinner rush). Impeccably dressed, unmistakably European, and with the rough-hewn good looks of a former great athlete (before he got his first jobs in the restaurant world, he was a world-class skier in his home country of Switzerland; he still swims several miles in the Atlantic Ocean beyond his Montauk, Long Island, home as often as possible), Briguet is immediately besieged by the maitre d', the bartender, and several waiters. Many of them, at one point or another, worked at one of Briguet's restaurants.

"Now this is a restaurant!" exclaims Briguet to nobody in particular. "You know," he says to the bartender, "I used to work here." In the 1950s, Briguet was a waiter in this very room—before it was La Côte Basque. He kisses Clark's hand, gives Lape a bear hug and series of bone-jarring slaps between the shoulder blades, and finally turns to me: "You're writing a book? Fantastic! I have some things to tell you!"

When Rachou finally appears, the contrast with Briguet

couldn't be more stark: Rachou is modestly dressed, a seemingly meek man with tousled gray hair. Throughout the meal, he describes himself repeatedly as "just a cook," which from his demeanor almost seems believable save for the reality that he is one of the most successful and sophisticated chefs and restaurateurs in American history. Indeed, while the closing of La Côte Basque is the big story on everybody's mind, Rachou is already plotting his next venture: a grand belle époque brasserie in the same location.

Lape, who matches Briguet's impeccable tailoring thread for thread, pokes fun at Rachou: "Do you really need to open another restaurant?"

Rachou fires back: "I didn't need to do it the first time." He is by all accounts a wealthy man. He could easily retire and live out his days in luxury. Instead, he chooses to live them out behind the stoves at a new restaurant. To me, this is emblematic of the best aspects of the restaurant business: the passion, the dedication, the striving for excellence whatever the cost.

While the others speak, a busboy sidles up to the table with a bread basket. After serving the rest of us, he puts a roll on Rachou's plate. Rachou touches the roll and, before the busboy can take a step away, he whispers a command in French. Plates are cleared. New bread arrives. Apparently our rolls were not to Rachou's liking. He suggests a foie gras terrine as an appetizer, and before anybody can indicate assent the order is placed.

In the postwar era and into the 1970s it was a given that fine dining was all about classic French cuisine. "It wasn't about creativity or inventiveness," explains Lape. "It was about who could cook the classic repertoire of Escoffier the best. You could go to a restaurant and judge it based on the execution of classic dishes." But all that started to change in the 1980s and 1990s, when American cuisine came into its own. Not that American cuisine, as distinct from its European origins, is particularly easy to define— but there is no dissent from the general proposition that there has been a departure.

Though as a typical New Yorker I always assume my city is the center of the universe, the reality is that the earliest stages of the new American culinary movement came out of California, which was traditionally less captive to European cuisiniers. A generation of California chefs, most notably Alice Waters, developed a focus on ingredients, seasonality, and regionalism that today is the predominant way of thinking among the most popular chefs and food writers. This movement in California paralleled the movement toward lighter nouvelle cuisine in France, but it had a unique American spin, a sense of freedom and possiblity. Rachou, Briguet, and their ilk, whose culinary roots go back to the era before nouvelle cuisine or California cuisine, were largely unaffected by the new aesthetic, though they did benefit from the increased availability of better ingredients.

Over the course of several hours, beginning with drinks and ending with cigarettes (in remorseless violation of city codes) and digestifs after midnight in an empty dining room, Rachou, Briguet, Lape, Clark, and I discuss the primary points of differentiation and evolution in restaurants during the latter part of the twentieth century.

To begin with, Rachou suggests, there was the education of great American cooks and the birth of great American chefs. Indeed, Clark comments, "In the 1960s and 1970s, almost nobody knew the names of any working restaurant chefs." It's difficult to imagine, in the era of Food TV, a time when chefs were largely anonymous, but a restaurant customer in the 1960s was more likely to know the name of the maitre d' than the chef, and to focus on the front of the house as the driving force in a restaurant. The whole concept of the "chef-driven restaurant," while the norm at the apex of dining today, is something very modern.

A moment of frisson occurs when Briguet suggests, "The Americans, they have the technical skills, but they don't have the palate."

Rachou fires back, "Come on Georges. American cooks are the best. How many French cooks do you have in your kitchen today?"

Briguet, after a pause, laughs heartily and shouts "None!" while almost knocking Rachou out of his chair with a slap between the shoulder blades.

As they talk, I listen—and eat. Just as I'm thinking to myself that Rachou's foie gras terrine is the best I've had in my life, the words "the best I've ever had" issue forth from Briguet in reference to the same dish. And I consider, as I dine with the chef while eating his food, the role of the chef. Surely the romantic notion of the chef as an individual artist who personally cooks all your food cannot be sustained when he is right there at the table with you while waiters are bringing hot food out of the kitchen. Having visited so many restaurant kitchens and seen them operate under the supervision of excellent sous-chefs, to me the romantic notion seems absurd.

Yet many people nonetheless feel that chefs should be in their restaurants, should have only one restaurant, and should at least be involved in every meal service. Throughout the food media and my e-mail inbox, people can be heard decrying the "absentee chef." To my way of thinking, however, all chefs are absentee chefs. The only variable I have been able to isolate is the extent of their absence.

At nearly any restaurant, the chef cooks a very small percentage of the food, if any. He is essentially absent from the cooking process, even if he is in the kitchen. As a supervisor, he can only see so many things happening at once. Likewise, in most restaurants, chefs have days off.

When a chef ascends to the level at which he has more than one restaurant, as a chef like Jean-Georges Vongerichten or Nobu Matsuhisa has, his level of absence increases. But it is simply an increase, not a fundamental shift in what he has been doing all along. The people who ran the kitchen on his days off now need to run the kitchen more often, and do more. The same cooks are cooking the food, however, and it is the same chef at the top of the organizational pyramid—the pyramid is simply larger. Some chefs can pull it off and some can't. If a chef's kitchen slips when he's away from it for a couple of days, that is his personal failure as a chef.

It is not even strictly necessary for a restaurant to have just one chef. There is a long tradition in France of having co-chefs, such as the father and son team of Michel and Jean-Michel Lorain at La Côte St. Jacques in Burgundy. In the United States, the acclaimed Blue Hill restaurants in New York have had co-chefs since opening day. Most remarkably, after receiving every accolade and honor for ADNY, Alain Ducasse announced in 2004 that Didier Elena would be leaving the restaurant to be replaced by one of America's top French chefs, Christian Delouvrier, who would serve as Ducasse's co-chef. Already the recipient of four *New York Times* stars at Lespinasse, and formerly the chef at Les Celebrites (the previous occupant of ADNY's space), Delouvrier is A-list in terms of both his American and his French credentials.

The modern chef, who is likely to operate more than one restaurant in a corporate fashion as opposed to a stand-alone family business, is neither cook nor supervisor, but is rather an executive. Like any executive in any industry, the chef is judged in large part by his or her ability to make the big decisions and delegate the rest. Just as Escoffier brought the modern industrial concept of the assembly line into the world of the restaurant kitchen, chefs like Vongerichten, Matsuhisa, and, of course, Alain Ducasse have been the leaders in bringing modern management into haute cuisine restaurants.

Cooking is, moreover, much more of a collaboration than many would like to let on. It's a collaboration not just between executive chefs and their top assistants, but also between chefs and suppliers, chefs and sommeliers, chefs and pastry chefs, chefs and customers, chefs living and chefs long gone. What you eat in the best restaurants today is largely a result of teamwork.

There are a handful of very small restaurants in the world—I've written here about Sandor's in Seagrove Beach, Florida—where the chef does cook most every dish. Such restaurants are atypical and idiosyncratic. But even in those cases, there are absences. At Sandor's, for example, the cold plates are prepared to order by the waitstaff while Sandor Zombori cooks the hot food. And, of course, Sandor didn't grow the vegetables, raise the animals, and mill the wheat or even bake the bread served at his restaurant.

What is on your plate, even if cooked by Sandor, represents much that has happened in Sandor's absence.

To me, the test of a restaurant is not the presence or absence of its chef, but the quality of its food. And given all the effort, by so many people at so many stages of a beautifully elaborate process, that goes into making that food, I believe it deserves to be the focus.

Rachou continues our discussion of the evolution of American cuisine by pointing to the increased availability of high-quality domestic ingredients. "Forty years ago," he says, "you couldn't get nothing here!" Briguet tells a story of waiting on the first *New York Times* restaurant reviewer, Craig Claiborne. Claiborne said to Briguet, "Bring me whatever fish is fresh." Briguet replied, "Monsieur, you know as well as I do there's not a fresh piece of fish in the whole city." The same was true of most vegetables, and both Rachou and Briguet recall with discomfort the days of dumping boxes of frozen vegetables into blenders to make mysterious purees. "Besides high-quality meats and a few things in season," recalls Lape, "back then even at the finest restaurants you ate worse produce than you can get at any supermarket today."

At the same time, traditionalists like Rachou and Briguet have never embraced the California-derived attitude that "the ingredients should speak for themselves." Surely, ingredients should "speak," but they believe, and I agree, that often what makes cuisine something special is the added human element. It is, after all, the job of the chef to do something with ingredients.

I particularly reject the notion that "fresh, seasonal, and local" ingredients are always best. Objectively, they are not. And rarely does a restaurant advertising the fresh-seasonal-local formula actually get all its ingredients locally. It is more likely that a few prominent elements of a few heavily advertised chef's specialties will come from the local harvest, while the rest of the menu will be built on a base of trucked- and flown-in products. Even at Gramercy Tavern, where so much produce is purchased from the local farmers' market in season, there is half a year from November until May when fresh produce comes from elsewhere. And if the majority of products on a menu are to be transported from afar, I think it makes sense not to live in denial but to embrace the wonders of modern shipping and to focus on acquiring whatever is best in and of itself, not whatever is simply being offered up by the nearby soil at a given time.

Ingredients alone, then, have not propelled American cuisine forward—there has also been a human element. In this respect, traditionalists like Rachou and Briguet have something in common with the most cutting-edge chefs in the fusion and avant-garde movements. They focus on human intervention in the flavor and texture of ingredients, rather than letting the ingredients speak for themselves.

Such a discussion involves a small subset of restaurants, but they are the restaurants that drive cuisine forward. As in any art, there is a vanguard of tastemakers whom the rest look to for inspiration. Clark and Lape both observe, in this regard, that there are three types of restaurants. At the most basic level, the vast majority of restaurants serve the function of nourishment. They provide people with an alternative to cooking at home. Then there is a much smaller group of restaurants, where the emphasis is not on eating but on dining. These restaurants provide a meal experience that is not substitutionary but, rather, an event in and of itself. Finally, there are a few restaurants, perhaps a handful in every generation, that transcend mere dining and become a part of culinary history.

In recent years, many of the historically significant restaurants, especially those in the fusion and avant-garde movements, have focused on creativity and excellence beyond the traditional borders and categories. Beginning with the fusion cuisine movement in the 1980s and 1990s, kitchens in North America and Europe were opened up to Asian and Indian as well as Central and South American ingredients and influences.

Gray Kunz, Jean-Georges Vongerichten, and Nobu Matsuhisa are three of the leading figures in the development of what we now call fusion cuisine. Fusion cuisine, which is in many ways the culinary equivalent of postmodernism, brings together the ingredients and techniques of the East and West, often with mixed results when practiced by a less than brilliant chef. But the kitchens of the best fusion practitioners are able to execute complex combinations with seeming effortlessness. Many of Gray Kunz's creations at the old Lespinasse, for example, featured upward of twenty ingredients from around the world and would pass through the hands of five different cooks on the way to the dining room. Yet the end result was always a fully integrated product—something that, despite massive engineering in the kitchen, was not at all difficult to consume. The cuisine of the best fusion chefs, moreover, is subtle.

Of course, we also have the success of the best fusion chefs to blame, in part, for the recent proliferation of mediocre fusion restaurants. In the wrong hands, the tools of fusion cuisine can be responsible for some truly awful concoctions. An inexperienced chef who has not yet mastered the classics has no point of reference and will likely create dishes that are often more shocking than good.

More recently, a movement toward the culinary avant-garde has emerged. The spiritual leader of this movement is Ferran Adria, the famed chef of El Bulli restaurant in Spain. That neither fusion nor the culinary avant-garde came out of France is telling: "Spain is the new France" read the cover of the *New York Times Magazine*, discussing Adria's influence.

Some describe the cuisine of Ferran Adria and his disciples as an expression of "deconstruction." And it is true that in a sense the avant-gardists are about freeing ingredients and cuisine from traditional forms and transforming them into often surprising creations. But the use of the term deconstruction in discussions of Adria has always seemed curious to me, because I've never seen a true intellectual or spiritual connection between Adria's food and the philosophical and literary work of Jacques Derrida and Paul de Man. The word deconstruction as commonly used in the food media—and indeed it's a handy word for breaking down anything into its theoretical components—has little to do with deconstruction writ large. At the most basic level, deconstruction in the literary world is not a way of writing, it is a form of criticism. Without getting deep into the semantics of it all, to me deconstruction in the culinary world cannot come from chefs—it has to come from critics saying things like, "There is no inherent superiority of El Bulli over McDonald's." (And this has indeed, absurdly, been argued.)

The more colloquial use of deconstruction—meaning to analyze the components of a dish and rebuild them into something else—is simply what chefs have always done. I don't see a real difference between making potatoes into foam (as Adria has done) and turning wheat into bread. Pretty much all cooking is about transformation. Whether the end result is familiar is a completely different issue. Remember that what Adria is trying to do (and I will use Adria as shorthand for the avant-garde movement in cooking) is extract the essence of flavor from food and present it in a stimulating form. In other words, he's trying to make food taste good by escaping the prison of form and focusing instead on flavor, texture, and temperature. It is no surprise that pastry chefs are the community that is most especially accepting of this approach; it's much like what they do every day. Save for the occasional use of fresh fruit, pastry is all about transformation and the essence of flavor. There's no big piece of animal muscle or a whole bird or an asparagus spear to preserve.

Conservatism in art, music, literature, and cuisine plays an important role in preserving tradition. It's not just the natural order of things—society depends on conservatism as a tool of self-perpetuation—but it's also the best way to make a lot of people good at something. Most chefs would be better off following the formulae of the haute cuisine masters. There are schools to teach it, and the distribution of ingredients and the design of kitchens are aligned to support it. Most chefs lack the skill set to depart in any meaningful way from the orthodoxy and still make delicious food. But some do, and they should be celebrated.

Chefs still have to survive by making food that tastes

good. The whole point of the Adria strategy, as I see it, is to use the technology available to us to make food taste, feel, smell, and look its best. If some modernist chefs are guilty of cooking dishes with reckless disregard for flavor just to prove the point that something can be done, I reject that approach as self-satisfying and ultimately detrimental to the craft. But if they are trying to make delicious food, I don't want to deny them any avenue of expression—even if it means I have to re-educate my palate.

In the United States, Grant Achatz of Alinea in Chicago is one of the torchbearers of the culinary avant-garde. Another, the foremost disciple of Ferran Adria in America today, is the Washington, D.C.–based chef Jose Andres. When I visited three of his restaurants, Café Atlántico, Zaytinya, and Jaleo, I realized that Jose Andres is one of the most significant chefs in America today. A year later when I visited his boutique restaurant, Minibar, I had to alter my assessment of Jose Andres: he is one of the most significant chefs in the world. I have never, in the space of just a couple of hours, been exposed to so many flavor possibilities and such a diverse array of culinary stimuli. It was one of my most memorable meals.

It's not difficult to understand why Andres hasn't gained the recognition he so heartily deserves. He practices in Washington, D.C., a town the gastro-elites have designated as firmly second-tier; he doesn't have a fancy restaurant to his name; and his food is "weird." More importantly, the community of critics is ill-prepared to deal with culinary avant-gardists like Andres and Achatz. Their cuisine doesn't fit into neat categories; they are too handily (and incorrectly) dismissed, marginalized, or bracketed as derivative of Adria; and the plodding structural needs of today's restaurant reviews—a thumbs-up/thumbs-down dish-by-dish approach to analysis, certain expectations of luxuriousness and comfort at different price points and levels of culinary sophistication, and easy comparisons to commonly understood flavors and preparations—are not well served by the avant-garde approach. What I've seen written about Andres, Achatz, and Adria in the main-stream food press—even when it has been very positive—has been reminiscent of someone dedicated to Renaissance portraiture attempting to use the same language to evaluate Picasso. A new set of critical tools will be required to explain them.

Food is not all that has changed about dining in America. Another fundamental shift in the restaurant world, cited by Shelley Clark, has been the decline of formality in dining. She argues (and I agree) that, for instance, putting on a necktie is more than just a sartorial gesture. It is a sign of respect for an institution. It brings every customer in a restaurant into a community and generates an infectious celebratory and luxurious ambience. "Today," bemoans Briguet, "people don't know the rules." I haven't the heart to tell him that it's because, today, there are no rules.

Rachou also points out that economic factors are responsible for much of the evolution, as well as destruction, of fine-dining establishments in the past half-century. He sees a catch-22 in the restaurant business, an ever-upward spiral of cost and luxuriousness that makes the high end of dining more inaccessible and elite even as standards of dress and formality decline and restaurants become more about meal replacement. Costs of labor, insurance, and real estate are ever increasing, and I sense the chefs' feelings of being trapped. "If I didn't have the world's most generous landlord," says Briguet, "I could kiss my ass goodbye."

Listening to Briguet and Rachou, I marvel at how far we've come since those days of frozen vegetables and kitchens that all seek to emulate the same dishes. Yet there are many in the food world who are against change, or who take positions that effectively place them in opposition to culinary progress. Represented in part by the Slow Food movement, but also by mainstream food magazines like *Saveur*, they advocate traditional recipes above all others, oppose most internationalism in cuisine, and tend to scoff at the avant-garde. They advocate, to use the popular buzzword, "authenticity." (*Saveur* trumpets the words "Savor a world of authentic cuisine" on the cover of every issue.) Despite allowances made for some evolution, authenticity as commonly understood refers to the preservation of "original" recipes, presented with some historical and cultural context. In the language of Merriam-Webster's first definition, authentic means "conforming to an original so as to reproduce essential features."

While I'm all for preserving traditional recipes, like Rachou's cassoulet, the authenticity brigade has gone too far. Preserving tradition and allowing for progress are not mutually exclusive, and both are important to progress in the arts. Yet, in the food world, the authenticity police are everywhere these days. Have you ever dined in an Italian restaurant with friends who have just returned from Italy? "Oh, in Italy they never serve pasta as a main course," they'll inevitably say. Or, "Cappuccino after dinner? That would be unthinkable in Italy." (Amanda Hesser built a book on that premise.) Or, "You call this bolognese?" (There is nothing like a week in Europe or Asia to activate the authenticity chromosome.)

This attitude stands in stark contrast to the basic facts of human history: Italian cuisine did not spring into existence as a fully formed entity. There was no tomato sauce and there were no sun-dried tomatoes until centuries after the tomato first reached Europe from the New World, thanks to Christopher Columbus. When that beloved red fruit first appeared in Italy, did the local food cognoscenti protest, "We don't use these things in authentic Italian cuisine"? (If they had protested tomatoes, it would have been because tomatoes were originally thought to be poisonous.) And anyway, the chef preparing the "red sauce" could easily be a Mexican who started his day with a bagel and a schmear.

We could just as easily imagine knee-jerk authenticity-based complaints about chiles in China's Sichuan province, chocolate in France, and wine in Australia. If you dug really deep, you'd probably find that at some point in prehistory the very notion of cooking beasts over a fire instead of eating their bloody haunches raw was scorned for its inauthenticity, too.

Since everything in the world of food likely had some precursory experience, wouldn't it be smarter for us to make allowances for what "authentic" really means? If you ask me, such tolerance is necessary when you dine out in America. Many of the top chefs seem to collectively scoff at the maintenance of traditional cuisines. Jean-Georges Vongerichten and Gray Kunz run roughshod over culinary borders with the audacity of international arms dealers. Nobu Matsuhisa blends Peruvian, Japanese, and even seemingly extraterrestrial flavors together. Wylie Dufresne of New York's WD-50 presses oysters into paperlike sheets. Mario Batali cooks his pizzas on a griddle.

I believe these cooks demonstrate that authenticity isn't a repetition of history. Real authenticity, to me, is grounded in being faithful to oneself. This is the last definition given by Merriam-Webster, but to me it is the most appropriate for cuisine: "true to one's own personality, spirit, or character." That's why, despite their breaks with tradition, there's nothing inauthentic about the cuisines of the fusion chefs or the avant-garde chefs. Change for its own sake is phony, but true originality is authentic. And what great chefs eschew in terms of historical fealty, they make up many times over in originality: the big-name cuisiniers we hear so much about are just the most prominent soloists among a chorus of thousands of unsung chefs at every kind of restaurant from the traditional Little India curry shop to the postmodern dessert bar.

Certainly, when cooking off the grid, there's an element of risk that's not present when cooking from *Le Guide Culinaire*. Then again, Escoffier wrote in a different time and place—he didn't work with American ingredients, he didn't work with a cooking brigade from Latin America, he probably, as has always been the case with most French gastronomes, couldn't stand the slightest hint of hot pepper. What, then, is so authentic about a chef in San Francisco, who was perhaps born in Toledo, cooking from Escoffier's playbook?

And so, in thinking about how to rescue authenticity from the Smithsonian and use it as a living concept that supports excellence, it appears there is something common to the best inauthentic, polyglot, mutt-like, joyous American restaurants: a sense of self-reliance, self-confidence, and conceptual independence and integrity that comes more from Ellis Island than from the restaurants of Paris, Florence, or Tokyo.

Will the twenty-first century be the American century for cuisine? It's too early to tell, and it would be foolish to count the French out prematurely. France is still the dominant force in Western cuisine, with more of the world's best restaurants than any other nation and with stronger representation in fine dining than any other nation worldwide. Though classic French restaurants are a dying breed, virtually all of the top restaurants in major American cities are still very much French-influenced, and most still have European-born chefs.

Still, one cannot help but think that if there is a future for fine dining it will have its epicenter in the New World rather than the Old. If the opening of the Time Warner Center in New York does not herald the dawn of the American century in cuisine, at the very least it represents one of the most significant moments in American restaurant history, a moment of critical mass. It is a changing of the guard, and a potential renaissance. As Lutèce and La Côte Basque turn out their lights, several of the most ambitious restaurants ever are opening. The culture reinvents itself, in newer and, we hope, better ways.

We can do our part. As civilians, we can further the restaurant culture by developing an attitude of partnership with those in The Life, wherein we work together toward the common goal of excellence. Through a better understanding of the inner workings of the industry and an appreciation of what it takes to bring great restaurants to us, we can identify and reward that excellence, and dismiss the rest. And through respect for all cuisines—be they traditional, ingredients-driven, fusion-oriented, or radically avant-garde—we can enrich our every meal.

Additional Sources of Food and Dining Information

Reading about food and dining isn't as fun as actually eating in restaurants, but it's a lot cheaper. If you've been bitten by the restaurant bug—and I hope I've facilitated that—you may wish to pursue some additional sources.

NEWSPAPER FOOD SECTIONS

For the dining obsessed, the local newspaper food section is an essential resource for restaurant news, features, and reviews. In addition, most of the major cities' newspaper food sections contain content that can be of interest whether you live in those cities or not, because most of the major papers think of themselves as national or international publications. The major food sections tend to be available online for free, and they mostly publish on Wednesdays. Beware, however: many of the articles revert into a paid archive after they've been online for twenty-four hours, so do your reading on Wednesdays if you want to do it for free.

Some of the best food sections are in the *New York Times* (www.nytimes.com), *Washington Post* (www.washpost.com), *Los Angeles Times* (www.latimes.com), *San Francisco Chronicle* (www.sfgate.com), and *Chicago Tribune* (www.chicagotri-bune.com). Those are the ones that, in my experience, many professional food journalists say they read religiously. In addition, there often is interesting and well-written din-ing-related material in the *Atlanta Journal-Constitution* (www.accessatlanta.com*), Boston Globe* (www.boston.com), *Charlotte Observer* (www.charlotte.com), *Miami Herald* (www.miami.com), *Philadelphia Inquirer* (www.philly.com), *Seattle Times* (www.seattletimes.com), and several of the New York papers other than the *New York Times*, such as the *New York Post* (www.nypost.com), *New York Daily News* (www.nydailynews.com), and New York Observer (www.ob-server.com). Internationally, there is strong English-lan-guage food writing particularly in Canadian and British newspapers, such as Montreal's *Gazette* (www.montreal-gazette.com) and London's *Observer* (London, www.ob-server.co.uk).

America has a rich tradition of alternative newsweeklies, like New York's *Village Voice* (www.villagevoice.com), St. Louis's *Riverfront Times* (www.riverfronttimes.com), and Atlanta's *Creative Loafing* (www.creativeloafing.com). These newsweeklies often contain offbeat and interesting dining coverage, especially with respect to ethnic and cheap-eats restaurants.

To help you locate full lists of American and international newspaper food sections and alternative newsweeklies, see "The Culinary Internet" below.

MAGAZINES

The national food magazines tend to focus on cooking and travel more than on restaurants, but most have occasional restaurant features as well as news-oriented restaurant coverage in their front sections. The better food magazines that offer restaurant coverage include *Gourmet* (www.epicurious.com), *Bon Appétit* (also at www.epicurious.com), *Saveur* (www.saveur.com), and *Food & Wine* (www.foodandwine.com). There is also terrific in-depth restaurant coverage in some issues of the *Art of Eating* newsletter (www.artofeating.com).

Some of the best magazine writing about food and dining, however, is not in the food magazines at all. It is in the fashion magazines. The fashion magazines, particularly *Vogue* (www.style.com) and *GQ* (www.gq.com), and to a lesser extent *Elle* (www.elle.com) and *Vanity Fair* (www.vanityfair.com), have a history of commitment to food writing. The travel magazines, such as *Condé Nast Traveler* (www.concierge.com) and *Travel & Leisure* (www.travelandleisure.com), have their fair share of restaurant coverage, particularly with respect to major new openings. Both the *New Yorker* (www.newyorker.com) and the *Atlantic* (www.theatlantic.com) also have occasional excellent restaurant coverage. Unlike the newspapers, however, the major magazines tend not to make all their content available for free online. They may offer selected articles, but for the full package you'll need to subscribe, usually to the print edition.

Many cities have weekly and monthly magazines devoted to local culture, news, and events, and these contain some of the most interesting insider reports on restaurant goings-on. *New York Magazine* (www.nymetro.com), in particular, has some of the most ambitious and comprehensive restaurant coverage of any periodical, and *Time Out New York* (www.timeoutny.com) is also a good resource for local restaurant information. These local magazines tend to put their content online for free.

The restaurant coverage in the *Wine Spectator* (www.winespectator.com) is often thoughtful and detailed, and the magazine is helpful to those who wish to learn about wine as well as for collectors who want to stay on top of the new releases and trends.

THE CULINARY INTERNET

The sands of the online food world are ever shifting, and no list of food Web sites remains current for long. As a result, I'll focus on a few of the more general sites that have relative permanence.

You've seen mention of the eGullet Society's Web site (www.egullet.org) in this book. I'm executive director of that organization and believe it is the leading food discussion site, with regional restaurant discussion forums covering most of the world and frequent guest appearances by top chefs, restaurateurs, and food writers. Another restaurant resource is the Chowhound discussion site (www.chowhound.com), which is especially strong on cheap-eats and ethnic cuisines.

A thorough and up-to-date listing of culinary Web sites can be found on the SauteWednesday site (www.sautewednesday.com). SauteWednesday will link you to the Web sites of chefs, food writers, newspapers, magazines, discussion forums, and broadcast media. The best collection of headlines from and links to dining coverage in alternative newsweeklies is in the "culture" section of a site maintained by the Association of Alternative Newsweeklies, called AltWeeklies (www.altweeklies.com).

The major search engines and Web indices, Google (www.google.com) and Yahoo! (www.yahoo.com), are good places to start if you're trying to find information about a specific restaurant. These days, it is rare for a major restaurant not to have a Web site or to participate in a larger site, like CitySearch (www.citysearch.com), that contains general information and sometimes menus.

RESTAURANT GUIDEBOOKS

The Zagat Surveys (*www.zagat.com*) are available for major cities in America and worldwide. Their invaluable restaurant telephone and address directories provide good local dining overviews, especially for newcomers. In Europe, the Michelin red guides (www.viamichelin.com) serve a similar function.

In many cities, there are one-of-a-kind local dining guidebooks, often prepared by a dedicated individual and sometimes only locally available or self-published. It's worth seeking these out in local bookstores anywhere you plan to do a lot of dining. New York is a hotbed of such guides, including Jim Leff's *The Eclectic Gourmet Guide to Greater New York City* (Menasha Ridge Press, 1998), Robert Sietsema's *Food Lover's Guide to the Best Ethnic Eating in New York City* (Arcade Publishing, 2004 revised edition), and *Meat Me in Manhattan: A Carnivore's Guide to New York* by the mysterious "Mr. Cutlets" (Gamble Guides, 2003). Some guides I've found to be reliable elsewhere are Jonathan Gold's *Counter Intelligence: Where to Eat in the Real Los Angeles* (LA Weekly Books, 2000), *Flavourville: Lesley Chesterman's Guide to Dining Out in Montreal* (Montreal, ECW Press, 2002), and Jane and Michael Stern's coast-to-coast guide, *Roadfood* (Broadway, 2002).

BOOKS ABOUT RESTAURANTS, CHEFS, AND DINING

Anthony Bourdain's *Kitchen Confidential* (Bloomsbury, 2000) is an outrageously entertaining look at some of the more unsavory practices that can occur behind the kitchen doors. William Echikson's *Burgundy Stars* (Little, Brown, 1995) is an insightful chronicle of a year in the life of a Michelin two-star restaurant in France that is striving for three, and Leslie Brenner's *The Fourth Star* (Clarkson Potter, 2002) tells a similarly inspiring American tale. Both Irene Daria's *Lutèce: A Day in the Life of America's Greatest Restaurant* (Random House, 1993) and Helen Studley's *Life of a Restaurant* (Crown, 1994) give valuable behind-the-scenes insight. Pierre Franey's *A Chef's Tale* (Knopf, 1994) is a personal account of American dining history, whereas Patric

Kuh's *The Last Days of Haute Cuisine* (Penguin, 2001) and Leslie Brenner's *American Appetite* are more general accounts.

The team of Karen Page and Andrew Dornenburg has produced five heavily researched books about the food world: *Culinary Artistry* (Wiley, 1996); *Dining Out* (Wiley, 1998), *Chef's Night Out* (Wiley, 2001), *The New American Chef* (Wiley, 2003), and *Becoming a Chef* (Wiley, 2003, revised edition). Michael Ruhlman's *The Making of a Chef* (Henry Holt, 1997) is a look at culinary school, and his *The Soul of a Chef* (Viking, 2000) covers chefs' development of their careers. Dawn Davis's *If You Can Stand the Heat: Tales from Chefs & Restaurateurs* (Penguin, 1999) is a collection of profiles of top chefs. Mimi Sheraton's *Eating My Words: An Appetite for Life* (Morrow, 2004) and Sirio Maccioni and Peter Elliot's *Sirio: The Story of My Life and Le Cirque* (Wiley, 2004) give inside looks at the lives of a major critic and restaurateur, respectively, and when read together shed much light on the critic-restaurateur dynamic.

Those should hold you for a while, while I work on the next one.

Bibliography

Ascher-Walsh, Rebecca. "Alain Ducasse: Ishtar, the Restaurant." *Fortune*, August 14, 2000.

Bahar, Zillah. "A High-Tech Maitre d'." *The Industry Standard*, March 22, 2001.

Barth, Stephen, David K. Hayes, and Jack D. Ninemeier. *Restaurant Law Basics*. New York: Wiley, 2001.

Bruni, Frank. "An Election Night Web Journal." www.NYTimes.com, November 2, 2004. http://forums.nytimes.com/top/opinion/readers opinions/forums/washington/anelectionnightweb journal/index/html

Bruni, Frank. "Eat Up, But Don't Tell Your Cardiologist." *New York Times*, June 30, 2004.

Bruni, Frank. "For a Classic, Another Shade of Elegance." *New York Times*, June 23, 2004.

Bruni, Frank. "The Magic of Napa With Urban Polish." *New York Times*, September 8, 2004.

Burros, Marian. "For Ducasse, a Bumpy Beginning." *New York Times*, August 9, 2000.

Central Intelligence Agency. *The World Factbook 2004*. Dulles, VA: Brassley's Inc., 2004.

Commerce Clearing House. "Taxes May Be Due on Tips Even If Employees Don't Report Them." July 23, 2001, http://hr.cch.com.

Cuozzo, Steve. "New Ducasse Has No Class." *New York Post*, July 26, 2000.

Fabricant, Florence. "Star French Chef Ducasse Is Heading to Manhattan." *New York Times*, March 15, 2000.

Gawker.com. "Frank Bruni Announced as NYT Restaurant Critic." April 8, 2004, http://www.gawker.com/topic/frank_bruni_announced_as_nyt_restaurant_critic_014888.php.

Gill, A. A. "Table Talk: The Ebury." *Sunday Times* (London), October 26, 2003.

Gill, A. A. "Table Talk: Corner on the Square." *Sunday Times* (London), October 10, 2004.

Grimes, William. "A Face Lift for a Polished Performer (The Zagat Effect)." *New York Times*, October 20, 1999.

——. "The Perfect Tempest: A Sneak Preview of Ducasse." *New York Times*, July 12, 2000.

Henley, Jon. "Michelin Man Tucks in to Critic Who Spilled Beans." *The Guardian*, April 23, 2004.

Herbst, Sharon Tyler. *The New Food Lover's Companion: Comprehensive Definitions of Nearly 6000 Food, Drink, and Culinary Terms*. New York: Barron's Educational Series, 2001.

James Beard Foundation Awards, 2004. http://www.jamesbeard.org/awards/index.php.

Jenkins, Steven. *Cheese Primer*. New York: Workman Publishing, 1996.

Kaminsky, Peter. "The Return of the Prodigal Chefs: Thomas Keller and Gray Kunz." *New York Magazine*, January 4, 2004.

Kaplan, Ron, et al. "The Alinea Project." http://www.egullet.org/alinea.

Kirchhoff, Sue. "Natural Beef Industry Might See Boost from Mad Cow Fears." *USA Today*, January 12, 2004.

Kuh, Patric. *The Last Days of Haute Cuisine*. New York: Penguin, 2001.

Maccioni, Sirio and Peter J. Elliot. *Sirio: The Story of My Life and Le Cirque*. New York: Wiley, 2004.

Merriam-Webster. *Merriam-Webster's Collegiate Dictionary, 11th Edition*. Springfield, MA: Merriam-Webster, 2003.

Miller, Bryan. *The New York Times Guide to Restaurants in New York City 1993–94*. New York: Times Books, 1992.

Montagne, Prosper (editor). *Larousse Gastronomique*. New York: Clarkson Potter, 2001.

National Cattlemen's Beef Association. "Davidburke & Donatella." *Veal Dish*, Winter 2003.

National Public Radio. "Father of 'Green Revolution' Derides Organic Movement." Interview with Norman Borlaug on *All Things Considered*, March 26, 2004.

National Restaurant Association. *2004 Restaurant Industry Forecast: Executive Summary*. Washington, D.C.: National Restaurant Association, 2004.

Niman Ranch. "Does Niman Ranch Sell Organic Meat?" http://store.nimanranch.com/store/nimanranch/help3.jsp.

North American Meat Processors Association. *Meat Buyer's Guide*. Reston, VA: North American Meat Processors Association, 2003.

Prial, Frank J., "Obituary: Roger W. Martin, 70, Restaurant Consultant." *New York Times*, January 13, 2003.

——. "Popping corks: A Sound Bound for Oblivion?" *New York Times*, May 15, 2003.

Rande, Wallace L. *Introduction to Professional Foodservice*. New York: Wiley, 1996.

Roberts, Paul. "The New Food Anxiety." *Psychology Today*, March–April 1998.

Rozin, Paul. "Food Is Fundamental, Fun, Frightening, and Far-Reaching." *Social Research*, Spring 1999.

Saad, Cindy. "From South Street Seaport to Southern Hunts Point." *Pace Press*, April 1, 2004.

Samburg, Bridget. "Read 'Em and Eat: The Zagats." *Brill's Content*, May 2000.

Schoeneman, Deborah. "Dueling Guides: French Invasion." *New York Magazine*, May 10, 2004.

Shaw, David. "Matters of Taste: They Have a File on You." *Los Angeles Times*, April 23, 2003.

Sheraton, Mimi. *Eating My Words: An Appetite For Life*. New York: Morrow, 2004.

St. John, Warren. "London Food Critics Have Knives Out for the Chefs." *New York Times*, November 9, 2003.

United States Department of Agriculture. "The Role of USDA's Beef Grading Program in the Marketing of Beef." http://www.ams.usda.gov/lsg/mgc/beefrole.htm.

United States Food and Drug Administration. "Guide to Inspections of Dairy Product Manufacturers." http://www.fda.gov/ora/inspect_ref/igs/dairy.html.

Vettel, Phil. "Holding Reservations About Us, Restaurants Fight Back Against No-Shows." *Chicago Tribune*, March 3, 1996.

Wiegle, Matt. "New Haven: The Birthplace of American Pizza." *Yale Herald*, Frosh Issue, 2000.

Williams, Ben. "The Critics Critiqued." *Slate.com*, December 31, 2003, http://www.slate.com/Default.aspx?id=2093333.

Zagat Surveys. *America's Best Meal Deals*. New York: Zagat Surveys, 1998.

———. *Chicago Restaurants*. New York: Zagat Surveys, 2003.

———. *New York City Restaurants*. New York: Zagat Surveys, 1997–2003.

Index

Index

Index